WITHDRAWN

SAN FRANCISCO BAY
SHORELINE ADVENTURES

BEST OF THE SAN FRANCISCO BAY TRAIL
AND BAY WATER TRAIL

———————

ACCESS MAPS TO THE ENTIRE
SAN FRANCISCO BAY AND WATER TRAIL

A San Francisco Bay Trails Press Book

Demece Garepis, *Author*
Tracy Cox, *Designer*
Ben Botkin, *San Francisco Bay Water Trail Planner*

San Francisco Bay Trails Press
San Francisco | Oakland | San Jose

San Francisco Bay Trails Press is a small publisher committed to sharing the cultural roots of contemporary trails around the San Francisco Bay Area for all to enjoy. San Francisco Bay Trails Press is an independent publisher informing the public of the San Francisco Bay and Water Trails Projects, and is not affiliated with the Projects.

San Francisco Bay Trails Press

San Francisco | Oakland | San Jose

Copyright 2021 by San Francisco Bay Trails Press

Although we have made every effort to be accurate, updates are inevitable in some routes and places described. We would appreciate your comments to help us keep this guide up-to-date. Contact us at sfbaytrailspress@gmail.com

Library of Congress Cataloging-in-Publications Data

San Francisco Shoreline Adventures: The Best of the San Francisco Bay Trail and Bay Area Water Trail/ Demece Garepis, author, {et.al.}

1st edition

p. cm

Includes bibliographical references and index.

ISBN 978-0-578-92594-3

    1. San Francisco Bay Area (Calif.)-Guidebooks. 2. Bay Trail and Bay Water Trail (Calif.)-Guidebooks.

Contents

vi Introduction – Welcome to Ohlone Land
1 How to Use this Book

North Bay

6   North Bay Map
8   Introduction to North Bay — Magnificent Funnel of Wind, Fog, and Tides
10 Angel Island/Tiburon Ferry
12 Sausalito
14 China Camp/McNears Beach
18 Petaluma River
20 Napa River
22 Point Pinole Regional Shoreline
24 Richmond Ferry and Richmond Bike Path

Central Bay

28 Central Bay Map
30 Introduction to Central Bay — Plankton: Guardians of the Aquatic Galaxy
32 National Marine Sanctuary Visitor Center
34 Fort Point to Pier 52

McNears Beach Promenade and pier

- **36** Embarcadero and Mission Creek Basin to India Basin
- **38** Candlestick Point State Recreation Area
- **40** Jack London Square and Brooklyn Bsain
- **42** San Leandro Marina and Tidewater Center
- **44** Crowne Beach and Encinal Beach

South Bay

- **50** South Bay Map
- **52** Introduction to South Bay — Salt and Marsh Grass: Deep Breath!
- **54** Coyote Point Recreation Area
- **56** Westpoint Harbor and Redwood City Marina
- **60** Foster City: Leo Ryan Park & Baywinds Park
- **62** Eden Landing
- **64** Coyote Hills Regional Park
- **66** Baylands to Dumbarton Bridge
- **70** Alviso Marina County Park

Bay Trail Cards

- **72-127** Official San Francisco Bay Trail Cards
  25 Map Cards with Trail Descriptions and Bay Map
- **128** SF Bay and Water Trail Resources
- **129** Acknowledgments
- **130** Index

CONTENTS | vii

Introduction

Welcome to Ohlone Land

Ohlone culture thrived for over twelve thousand years before the Missions. Local tribes met often to arrange marriages, trade, and celebrate life events. Today's recognized Ohlone tribes include the two historic and previously federally recognized tribe, Muwekma Ohlone Tribe of the San Francisco Bay with an enrollment of over 600 BIA documented members descended from Missions San Francisco, Santa Clara and San Jose; and Amah-Mutsun Tribal Band from Mission San Juan Bautista, as well as several family organizations such as the Association of Ramaytush Ohlone.

The central coast of California to the Santa Clara Valley comprised one of the most populated tribal lands in North America. If you look at climate, resources, and water, the Ohlone villages were stewards of paradise. We have much of what we see today because Ohlone continue their traditions as land stewards.

The map at the end of this section does not show all Ohlone tribal villages; in fact, no map can. Several villages were associated with each tribe. As tribes grew, they splintered off and became new tribes. From 1769 when the Spanish arrived to the end of the Gold Rush in 1855, Ohlone were kidnapped and taken as guides, enslaved and forced into labor of all kinds. Many tribal members were written in the mission records. Other tribes fled. Refusing to be enslaved, they were murdered throughout the eras of Spanish, Mexican and American colonization. Many tribes were not recorded. One tribe of 250 members was eliminated because they entirely refused to be involuntarily held.

From 1900 through today, Ohlone have risen in resiliency and power. Ohlone use traditional ecological knowledge to carefully manage plant and natural

Coyote Hills Regional Park and the South Bay Marshes

resources as their ancestors did. Ohlone are leading impactful cultural and environmental projects throughout the Bay Area. Amah Mutsun have established the Amah Mutsun Land Trust which preserves cultural and sacred sites and restores traditional landscapes. Muwekma Ohlone partner with the East Bay Regional Parks to teach tule boat building and bay restoration. Ramaytush partner with the Exploratorium to develop an online walking tour of the buried history of San Francisco and train youth to advocate on local government issues and cultural landmarks.

Throughout the Bay, Ohlone partner with Cal Fire to manage controlled burns to clean out the understory in the redwood forests. Ohlone use both traditional and contemporary stewardship skills. Ohlone also smudge the trees. Fire management is important because it makes trees healthier.

Ohlone were never "hunters and gatherers". Ohlone very intentionally managed landscapes to provide food resources for all wildlife as well as themselves. At first contact, the Bay Area was and continues to be a park like setting – this is not a random or coincidental vision. These landscapes were stewarded by Ohlone to achieve this benefit.

INTRODUCTION | ix

We acknowledge Ohlone ways and land and we also learn how to support their current goals directly. Amah Mutsun fight to preserve Juristac, a sacred site proposed to be turned into gravel mining. We also learn to support Ohlone youth leadership projects. Now is the time to get involved and support Ohlone work today.

These sites on the SF Bay and Water Trail give you the most unfettered observation of our unique cultural roots. We share a thriving heritage to honor our past and shape our future.

GET INVOLVED

http://amahmutsun.org/land-trust
http://protectjuristac.org
*https://native-land.ca/maps/
   territories/ohlone/*

RESOURCES

http://www.ramaytush.com
http://amahmutsun.org
http://muwekma.org
*https://sogoreate-landtrust.org/
   purpose-and-vision/*

Map: native-land.ca

Amah Mutsun Today

Juristac is the most sacred site of the Amah Mutsun. Private developers want to turn it into gravel mining. Go to *protectjuristac.com* to learn how you can support preserving this sacred site.

"As the next generation of the Amah Mutsun nation, we envision a future where our ancestral rights are respected and access to our sacred lands is restored."
— *Alexii Signona, Amah Mutsun Tribal Band / #protectjuristac*

Amah Mutsun Tribal Chair Valentin Lopez leads a ritual to smudge the fire managed area by burning dried sage, purifying the forest. Amah Mutsun partner with Cal Fire to use old and modern techniques to consciously steward the habitat and understory plants

HOW TO USE THIS BOOK

Use this handy guide for a spontaneous getaway, the well planned bay water trail adventure, or a car free nature exploration. These destinations are among the best places to hike, bike, paddle, walk, run, and observe wildlife.

We travel all around the Bay Area. We live here, we work here, and we are always ready for a new bay adventure! This book is divided into three sections – North Bay, Central Bay and South Bay. Each section recommends best destinations, resources to build your skills, and how to get involved.

Respecting wildlife is the best gift to give our future generations. When you see flocks feed along the marsh, please stay 150 feet away. Stay on the trails. Otter, seals, and whales need at least 300 feet of water distance from us so they can navigate their environment. Pack in, pack out and stay alert for any changing conditions to keep your adventure truly awesome for others to enjoy.

The San Francisco Bay Trail and its website *https://baytrail.org* offers public bay access from trails to boardwalks with over 360 miles in place! The San Francisco Bay Trail connects communities to parks, open spaces, schools, public transit, heritage landmarks, and bike trails. The San Francisco Bay Trail intends to connect over 500 miles of public pathways.

The Bay Area Water Trail and its website *https://sfbaywatertrail.org* offers non-motorized launching and landing sites for recreational users. The San Francisco Bay Water Trail offers over 500 miles of navigable tributaries, shores, and is the region's largest open space

The San Francisco Bay Trail and The Bay Area Water Trail are projects managed by the California Coastal Conservancy. Together the The San Francisco Bay Trail and the Bay Area Water Trail offer new connections to access private and public points from boardwalks to pathways. The San Francisco Bay Trail Alerts will give you up to date access and landmark destination points and its News & Events tab updates new trail connections.

This combination gives you the best shoreline adventures - including San Francisco Bay Trail Cards and useful websites!

Land's End

THE NORTH BAY

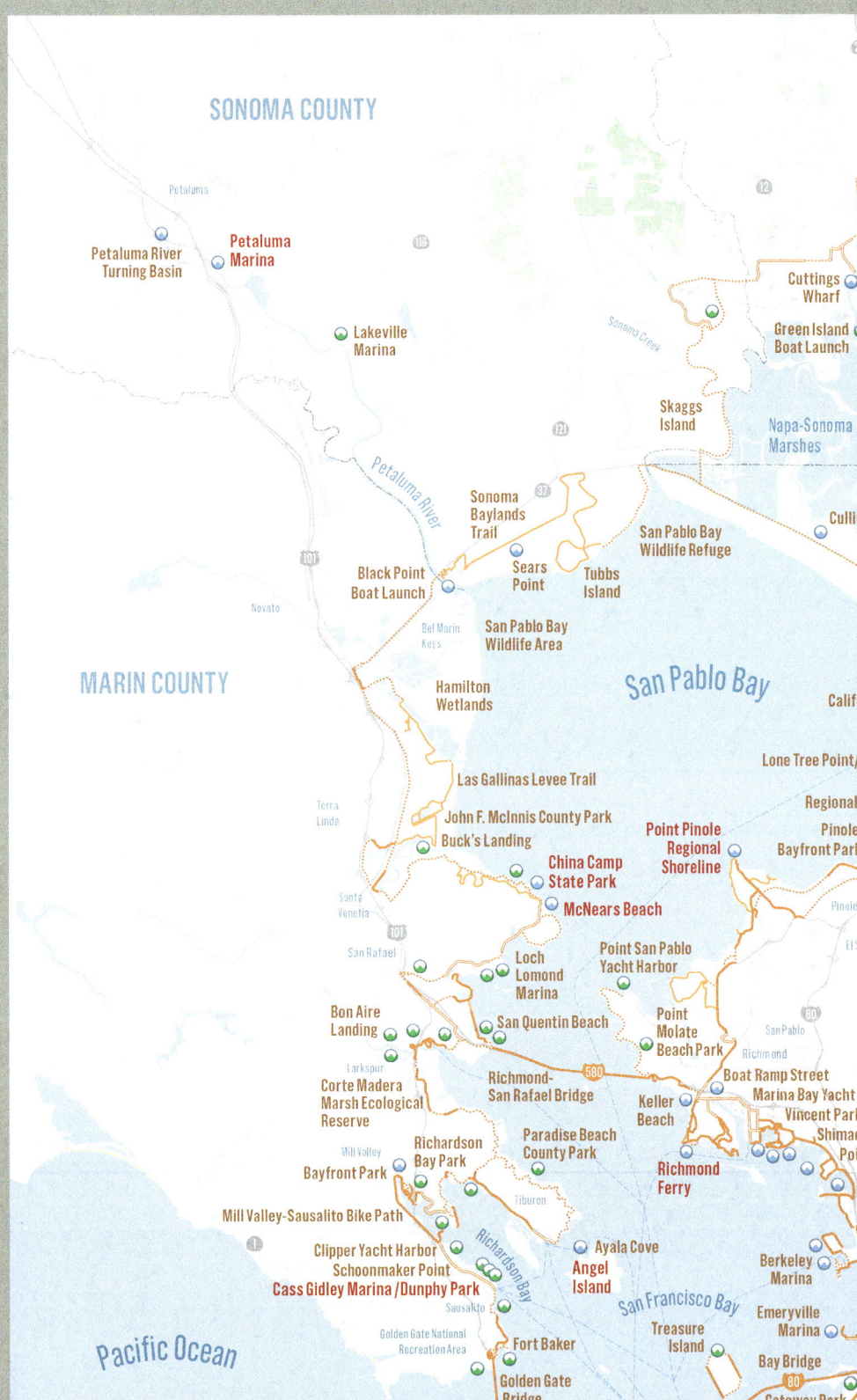

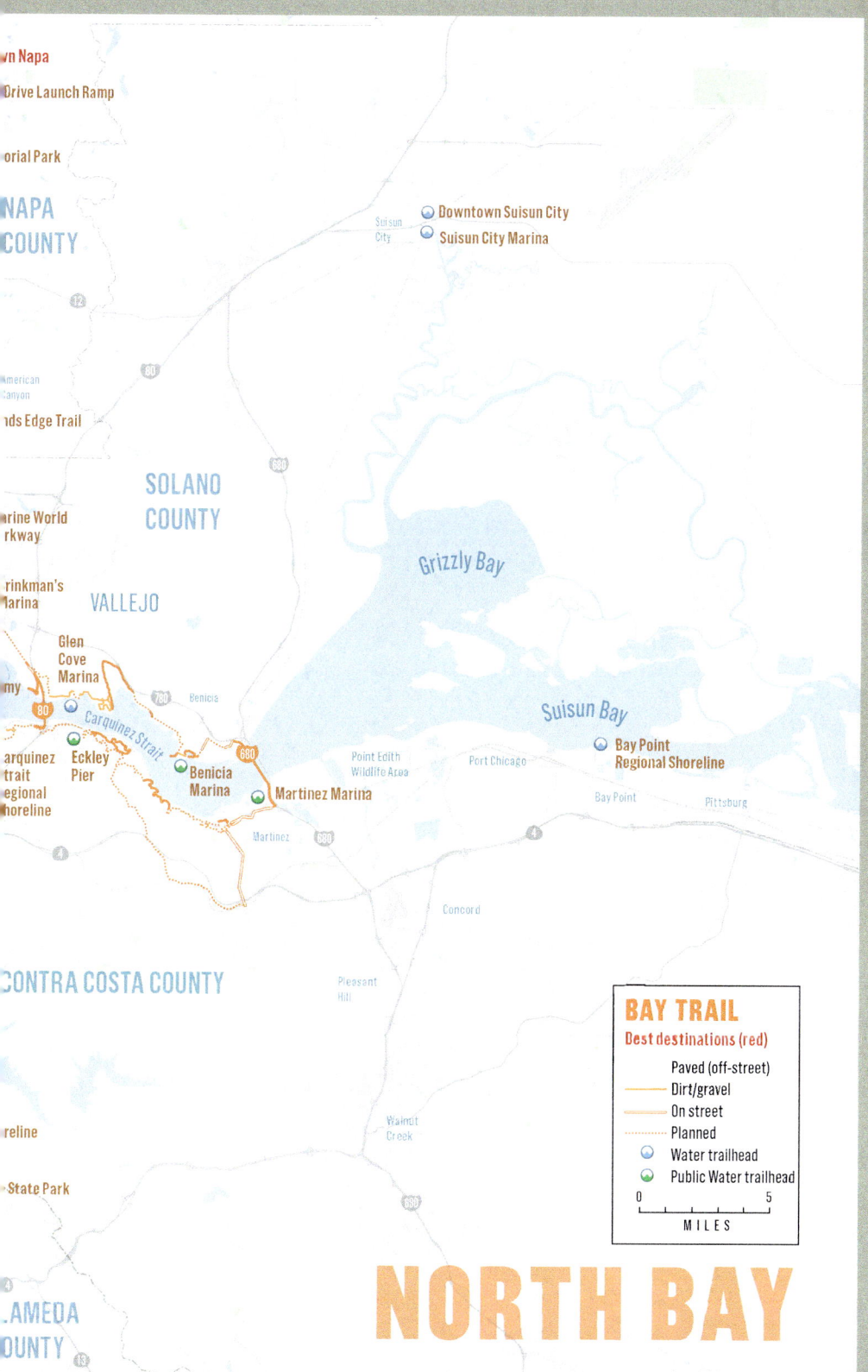

Paddling Petaluma River

Magnificent Funnel of Wind, Fog, and Tides

10 // *Angel Island/Tiburon Ferry*
12 // *Sausalito*
14 // *China Camp/McNears Beach*
18 // *Petaluma River*
20 // *Napa River*
22 // *Point Pinole Regional Shoreline*
24 // *Richmond Ferry and Richmond Bridge Bike Path*

Did you ever imagine the Golden Gate Bridge as a magnificent funnel? Our amazing fog, wind, tides and currents create a constantly dynamic funnel from the Delta to the Pacific. When paddling, use special caution where the current and tides can work for and against you – at the same time! The strongest air and water currents occur near Angel Island's over 160 foot undersea trench called Raccoon Strait or the 105 foot cliff Yellow Bluff, all around Alcatraz Island, and under the Golden Gate. As the tides change, so do current, ongoing sea traffic and prevailing wind and fog – the funnel never stops!

Did you know that all 8 types of fog can be found in the North Bay and the town with the most fog days on Earth is Point Reyes at 222 days a year?

FUN FACT

When you bike across the Golden Gate Bridge, you discover the raw panorama of the bay as the wind sets your pace. Trip planning is essential. Watch the weather and pick a trail that fits your style!. There is everyday fog called the marine layer, coastal fog, and there's also low-lying Tule fog – so many kinds of fog! Bring extra gear for changing conditions and have fun!

Angel Island & Tiburon Ferry

BAY TRAIL CARD 24

This adventure offers unparalleled panoramic views of San Francisco Bay. Spend the day on the Island! Travel by ferry or join a group paddle. Bike rentals are available at the ferry ports and on the Island. There are plenty of uncrowded easy to moderate level hiking trails. A tram tour of The Immigration Station, a National Historic Site, is recommended. Island overnight camping is available.

- *Ferries:* San Francisco, Sausalito, Larkspur, Tiburon to Ayala Cove, Angel Island State Park
- *Hike and bike* Angel Island: North Ridge and Sunset Loop, Angel Island Perimeter Trail, Sunset Trail to Mount Livermore, Mount Caroline, Livermore via North Ridge Trail
- *Paddle:* Cass/Gidley Marina to Ayala Cove, Dunphy Park Angel Island State Park Beach and Camping
- *Paddle Rentals and Tours:* Sea Trek

Angel Island Harbor and launch ramps

Top: Richardson Bay paddle to Angel Island. Left: Hiking and Camping on Mt. Livermore Peak. Above: Angel Island Beach and Tram Station. Bottom: Angel Island Trail view of the Bay

Sausalito

BAY TRAIL CARD 25

Sausalito's network of cozy public beaches offers a retreat for everyone, including bikers, hikers, and boaters. If you are curious about the boating community of Sausalito, look no further than **Cass Gidley Marina.** The Marina provides high and low dock ADA access in the calmer cover of Richardson Bay. Bike rentals are located in the parking lot. The Marina also offers live music. The Sausalito Community Boating Center is a great resource to learn boating skills and have access to affordable boats. Check out their annual Herring Festival – a unique bay music, food, and cultural event for everyone.

Dunphy Park is just around the corner from Cass Gidley Marina The newly expanded Dunphy Park extends the public shoreline path for biking, hiking, picnics, volleyball, bocce ball, beach and launch areas.

Schoonmaker Point Marina has a great little beach with an even greater resource to build your skills or tour the Bay. Bike rentals are available. Sea Trek is an oustanding paddle training and touring resource for everyone. Visit the Bay Model, built by the U.S. Army Corps of Engineers to demonstrate a working hydraulic model of the Bay Area Water Trail region from the San Francisco Bay to the Sacramento River Delta.

Turney Street Boat Ramp
Less than a mile away from Schoonmaker Point is Turney Street Boat Ramp which has a recently renovated public ADA launch and boat ramp to meet sea level rise predictions.

Dunphy Park Gazebo along the Bike Trail and Beach

Above: Sea Trek low dock ramp. Below: Turney Street Boat Ramp

China Camp & McNears Beach

BAY TRAIL CARD 21

China Camp preserves a historic Chinese shrimping community the Quan Family archives, and offers many accessible trails. Biking, hiking, swimming, picnicking, pier fishing, ADA grounds, and beach launch are all available at China Camp. This is a prime destination to celebrate the local culture, including the Chinese-American Heritage Day in August featuring lion dances, tai chi demonstrations, family activities, and a tour of the reconstructed shrimping boat the *Grace Quan*, named after Frank Quan's mother. It was John Muir's distant relative, also named John Muir, who saw a shimp boat trawling in the Bay and took on the job to build the *Grace Quan* using local redwood and traditional methods. o learn more about China Camp, go to *https://friendsofchinacamp.org*.

McNears Beach offers unparalleled views of San Pablo Bay. Tennis, kite flying, skateboarding, swimming, picnicking, pier fishing, ADA grounds and launch are all available in this warm and wind protected cove. It's a magical place for the whole family!

China Camp Beach has an easy launch, a warm shallow swimming beach cove and rental cabins

Top: China Camp pier and public fishing
Bottom: China Camp Bike Trails and Picnic Areas

"Getting involved locally is a rewarding way to ensure our watershed will be protected for generations to come."

— Ben Botkin, Bay Area Water Trail Planner

McNears Beach ADA launch

Top: McNears long pier for strolls and public fishing
Bottom: McNears Promenade and Trail

Petaluma River

BAY TRAIL CARD 19 & 20

This lovely river's name is derived from Miwok from peta (flat) and luma (back). Petaluma River flows into San Pablo Bay which makes it a rich environmental watershed. The Petaluma River Watershed encompasses over 247 miles of tributaries from the Sonoma Mountain to San Pablo Bay. This watershed is a great example of tidal and urban effects. You can see lots of tidal debris on the banks while still enjoying good water quality. The watershed drops into the salt marsh of San Pablo Bay, a significantly restored wetland. ADA launches at Petaluma downtown and Petaluma Marina offer accessible paddling all the way down the Petaluma Marsh to San Pablo Bay. Bike and hiking trails are along the Petaluma River and also in downtown Petaluma. Bike rentals are located throughout Petalama.

Downtown launch to Petaluma Marsh

Above: Petaluma's Annual Event "Day on the River" sponsored by Friends of the Petaluma River

Left: Downtown Petaluma offers low ramp launches

Below: Paddling the Petaluma Marsh to San Pablo Bay

Napa River

BAY TRAIL CARD 18

The Napa watershed – remember it's all about water -- encompasses over 462 miles of tributaries from Kimball Canyon Creek in Robert Louis Stevenson State Park to the amazingly diverse Napa Sonoma Marsh. The Napa River is a spawning ground for over sixteen native fish species – from steelhead trout to white sturgeon. The California Golden Beaver is also returning to its Napa River habitat. Re-exposing the water to daylight allows the river's ecology to thrive. The southern part of the river restores the salt ponds. Downtown Napa offers a variety of bike rentals.

The Napa River Promenade

Top: Napa River paddlers

Bottom: Kennedy Park low ramp launch and pier

Point Pinole Regional Shoreline

BAY TRAIL CARD 14

The Shoreline has all you need: unparalleled views of the Bay, ADA trails, picnic tables, easy beach launch, camping and great walking and biking trails, and an interesting history from being the site of a dynamite plant to supplying Disneyland. The Bay View Trail is an ADA trail, featuring an easy beach launch and a round trip shuttle to the pier. The pier is a prime spot for fishing and offers the most panoramic views of the Bay area. If it's quiet you seek, look no further than Owl Alley trail. Owl Alley, an open meadow trail lined with eucalyptus, is a popular birdwatching trail at sunset.

Point Pinole Regional Shoreline, Owl Alley Trail

Top: Bay View Trail

Center: Picnic and play area at Point Pinole Trail

Bottom: Bay View Trail

Richmond Ferry & Richmond Bridge Bike Path

BAY TRAIL CARD 23

Get out of traffic and ride the ferry! Take your friends and family on a day trip. Take the ferry from Richmond to the San Francisco Ferry Terminal, or as far north as Vallejo to as south as South Francisco. Weekday service is available and combine that with a Bay Land or Water Trail adventure! Bike rentals are available at the Ferry.

Be one of the first to cross the new 5 mile Richmond Bridge Bike Path. The San Rafael-Richmond Bridge has ample parking at either end. Bike rentals are available throughout Richmond and San Rafael. The Bridge Bike Path starts on Castro Street in Richmond, where barriers separate bikes from vehicular traffic all the way to San Rafael. If you do a one way trip, plan to start at the Richmond end so it's all downhill to San Rafael. You can count on wind, fog, and fabulous views - bring an extra layer of clothing to explore this bay crossing!

Richmond Ferry Terminal and Promenade

Top: Richmond Ferry Terminal

Bottom: Richmond Bridge Bike Path biking to the San Rafael exit

BUILD YOUR SKILLS

Sausalito
- Sausalito Community Boating Center
- Sea Trek

Petaluma
- Petaluma River Cruises: Dolphin Charters
- Clavey Paddlesports
- Friends of The River

San Rafael
- 101 Surf Sports

Napa
- Napa Valley Paddle

Richmond Marina
- REI Watersports classes

Bike Rentals available near all desinations

Top: Fort Point Bike Path
Center: Crowne Beach Windsurfers
Bottom: Heron's Head Park Trail

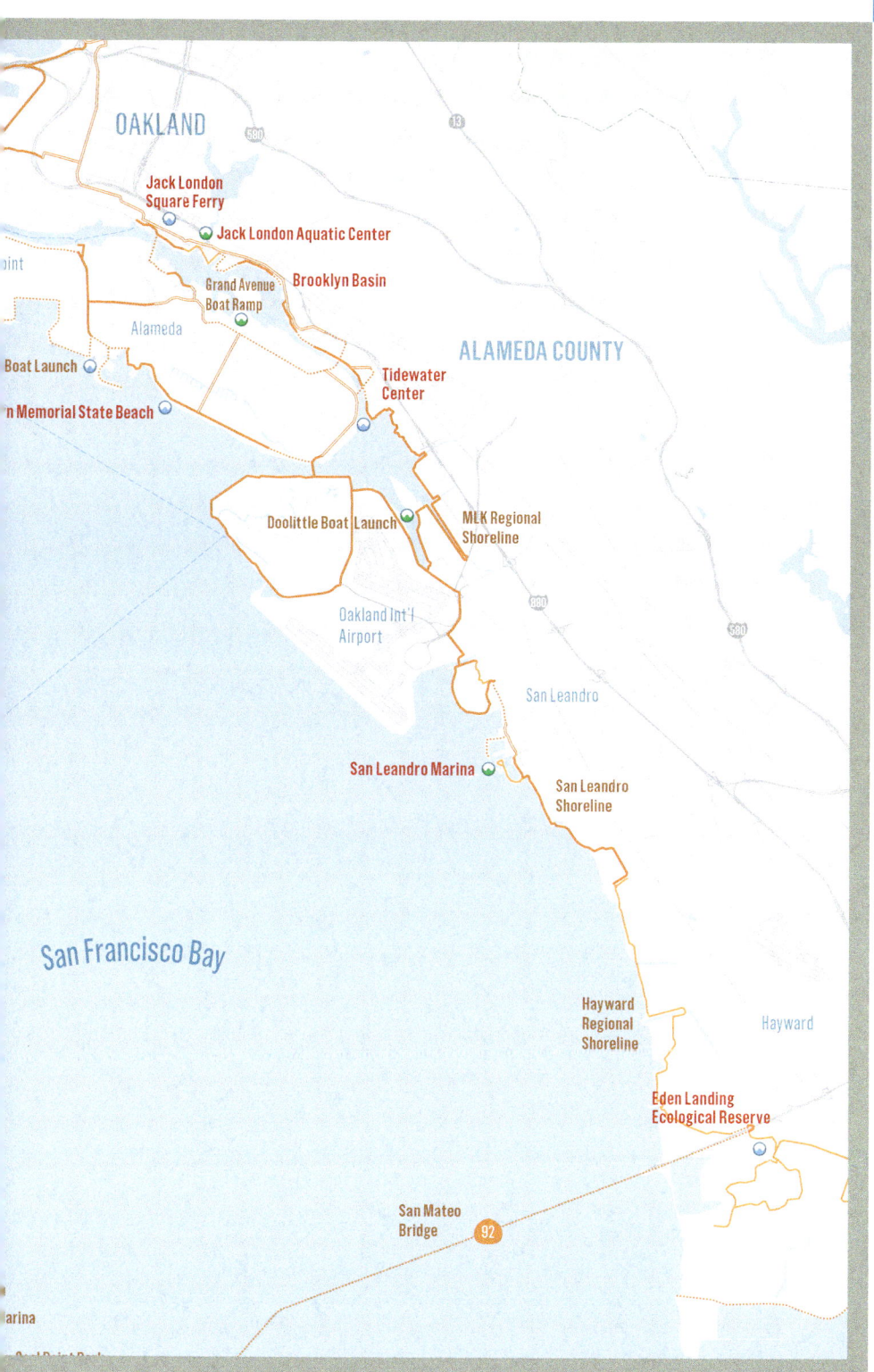

Porcelain Sand Crab plankton in the Bay

Top Right: Pacific Sand Crab in the zoea life stage

Botton Right: Noctiluca also known as sea sparkles

Plankton: Guardians of the Aquatic Galaxy

- 32 // *National Marine Sanctuary Visitor Center*
- 34 // *Fort Point to Pier 52*
- 36 // *Embarcadero and Mission Creek Basin to India Creek Basin*
- 38 // *Candlestick Point Recreation Area*
- 40 // *Jack London Square & Brooklyn Basin*
- 42 // *San Leandro Marina & Tidewater Center*
- 44 // *Crowne Beach and Encinal Beach*

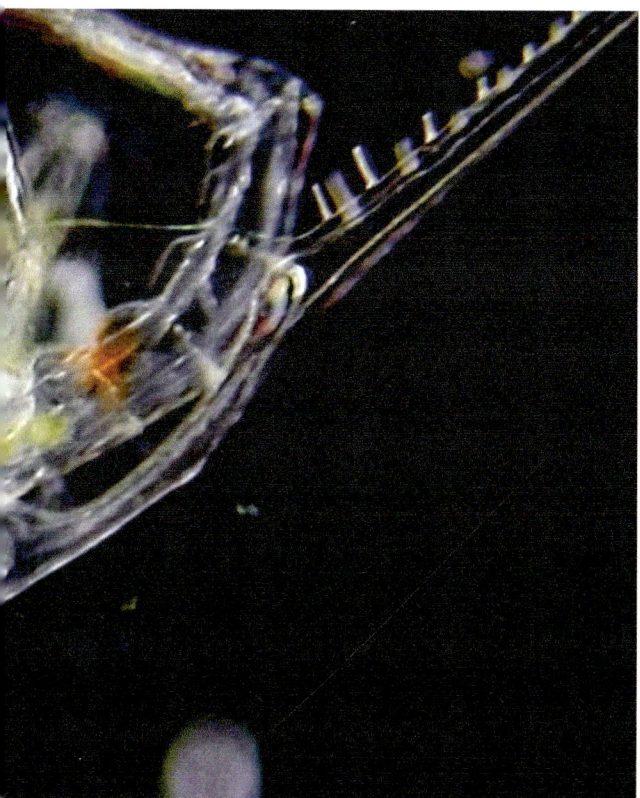
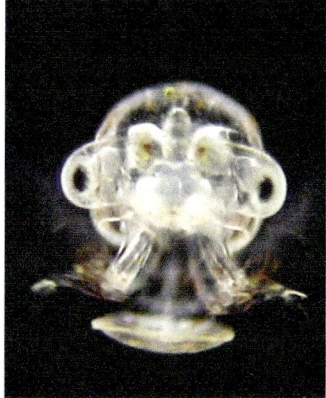

The San Francisco Bay supports one of the richest aquatic ecosystems in the world. Tide and sunlight enrich phytoplankton – the food network –for aquatic wildlife from starfish to whales. Plankton supply over 50% of our oxygen. How can they do that? Are they super heroes? Well, yes they do, and yes they are. Are you alive, in the water, and a drifter you're a plankton too! Plankton is more of a lifestyle than an organism. Some organisms are plankton their whole life, while others are guests of the planktonsphere, such as crabs, snails and worms. Noctiluca - the bioluminscent plankton - make their own light, and they stay plankton. Diatoms stay plankton too. Phytoplankton supply so much oxygen – only superheroes can do that!

Did you know the newly funded San Francisco Bay Restoration Act will help protect our bay from climate change by restoring wetlands, reduce pollution and support wildlife?

FUN FACT

Presidio: National Marine Sanctuary Visitor Center

BAY TRAIL CARD 1

The Greater Farallones National Marine Sanctuary Visitor Center located at the historic Coast Guard Station is a hidden gem and world class adventure. Center visitors can watch the whales and puffins on live cams from the Farallones. View the bay aquarium and take a peek at bay plankton under microscopes! Reserve your spot in advance to do family activities such as plankton retrieval and identification. The Visitor Center offers lots of educational resources about wildlife and conservation. *https:// farallones.noaa.gov/education/publicworkshops.html*

Greater Farallones National Marine Sanctuary Research Pier

Above, Visitor Center Activity: Looking at noctiluca and crab plankton through the microscope. Bottom Left: Marine Sanctuary Visitor Center Manager Justin Holl releases the plankton specimen jar from the plankton drift net.

"Some phytoplankton bump and light up their predators chasing them so they get eaten first!"

"There is so much to discover about plankton, what determines their adaptation from fresh to saltwater."

— Janai Southworth, Bay Plankton Scientist, National Marine Sanctuary

Fort Point to Pier 52

BAY TRAIL MAP CARD 2

Fort Point to Pier 52 is an amazing adventure. The Golden Gate National Recreational Area offers premier biking, hiking and amazing water sports.
Crissy Field holds world class wind surfing events, but you don't need to be a sports professional to enjoy all that Crissy Field offers. Bike and kayak rentals are available in the Presidio all the way to Pier 52. You can spend a quick picnic to a whole day on the beach. The walk or bike ride down to Pier 52 along the Embarcadero is one of the best views of the Bay you'll encounter. Along the way, explore the National Maritime Museum, Hyde Street Pier, Fort Mason, Aquatic Park, Pier 39, and the Exploratorium all the way to the Ferry Building!

Crissy Field Sup in the waves

Above: Crissy Field Promenade. Below: Aquatic Park Promenade

Embarcadero & Mission Creek to India Basin

BAY TRAIL CARD 2

The expanding mosaic of public access on the Embarcadero features lots of exciting adventures along the Mission Creek Watershed. You can hike, kayak, take a ferry, or bus to experience the vibrant neighborhoods of Mission Bay, Dogpatch and Bay View Hunters Point. Just to name a few, you can rent a kayak or sup at City Kayaks at Pier 40, and UCSF's Mission Creek Park boathouse offers skill building and rentals. You can always hop a ferry at Pier 39 or the Ferry Building and tour the Bay. Bike rentals are available all along the Embarcadero. The bike trail is a bit segmented but worth the meander along Embarcadero across Lefty O'Doul Bridge, passing Islais Creek to Warm Water Cove, Heron's Head Park and the Eco Center. Easy bay access

Heron's Head Bike Path

at Warm Water Cove were made possible by the Bay Conservation Development Commission that founded Bay shoreline public access. Work by the SF Port Commission from Embarcadero to the Bay View Hunters Point Shoreline is underway to unify bike, walk trails, and water access. Take time to check out the Museum of Craft & Design on Third Street, the cafes and amazing art studios in the Hunter's Point Shipyards.

Top: McCovey Cove Paddlers
Center: Embarcadero Promenade
Bottom: Warm Water Cove Park

Candlestick Point Recreation Area

BAY TRAIL CARD 2

From WW2 garbage dump to world class garden - Candlestick Recreation Area is California's first reclaimed land restoration area. Great place for fishing, dog walking, skateboarding, paddling and wind surfing. Spectacular views along the shoreline trails, a long urban beach, and plenty of picnic tables. A great place for urban hiking with links to the Crosstown Trail.

Paddling Candlestick Point to Hunter's Point Naval Shipyards

Top: Candlestick Point Beach. Center: Paddling toward Hunter's Point. Bottom: Candlestick Point Beach launch

Jack London Square & Brooklyn Basin

BAY TRAIL CARD 10

Engage in the cultural events going on at Jack London Square and combine it with a ferry at Jack London Square – and the result is a great adventure. Brooklyn Basin is a wonderful new place to join a bay tour at California Canoe & Kayak. Bike rentals are available at Jack London Square and Brooklyn Basin.

Brooklyn Basin Bladers

Above: Jack London Promenade. Below: Jack London launch ramp along the Promenade

San Leandro Marina & Tidewater Center

BAY TRAIL CARD 9

This marina is nestled in the calm southern tip of Oakland Estuary and a great place to head out to the Bay Bridge. The Marina provides over seven miles of biking and walking trails, inviting playgrounds, and a visitor center.
Located on the Martin Luther King Jr. Regional Shoreline, the Tidewater Center offers affordable boating and paddle skills and boat rentals for everyone.

Above: San Leandro Marina Public Boat Launch. Below: Tidewaters Center public launch

Top: Tidewaters Center and San Leandro Marina Promenade. Bottom: San Leandro Bike and Walk Trail

East Bay Regional Parks:
Crowne Beach & Encinal Beach

BAY TRAIL CARD 8

Known for its warm water and easy non motorized launch area, Crowne Beach is a great destination for swimming, paddling, and picnicking. Boardsports lessons and paddle rentals are also available. Crowne Beach also offers concerts and annual family events.

Tucked a half mile away in Crab Cove is Encinal Beach, a recently restored sandy beach and an adjacent cement boat ramp. This is a perfect beach for swimmers and anyone who wants to learn paddling. Get there early, since there is a free parking lot with a two hour time limit, and many fishing boats use the cement launching ramp. This is a lovely underused beach and shallow cove to view the brown pelicans and a seal haul outs from a safe distance.

Crowne Beach windsurfing skills session

*Above: Crowne Beach's shallow beach launch great for walking and water sports.
Below: Encinal Beach Promenade to the beach*

Above: Crowne Beach Trail. Below: Encinal Beach launch

BUILD YOUR SKILLS

Oakland:
- California Canoe & Kayak
- UC Berkeley Cal Adventures at Berkeley Marina
- Tidewater Boating Center

Alameda:
- Alameda Recreation and Parks Department
- Alameda: Mike's Paddle
- Alameda Community Sailing Center
- O'Kalani Outrigger Canoe Club
- Stacked Adventures

San Francisco:
- UCSF Outdoors Unlimited at Mission Creek
- Pier 40: City Kayak
- San Francisco State University
- Treasure Island Sailing Center
- Environmental Traveling Companions

Bike Rentals available near all destinations

Coyote Hills Regional Park marshes

THE SOUTH BAY

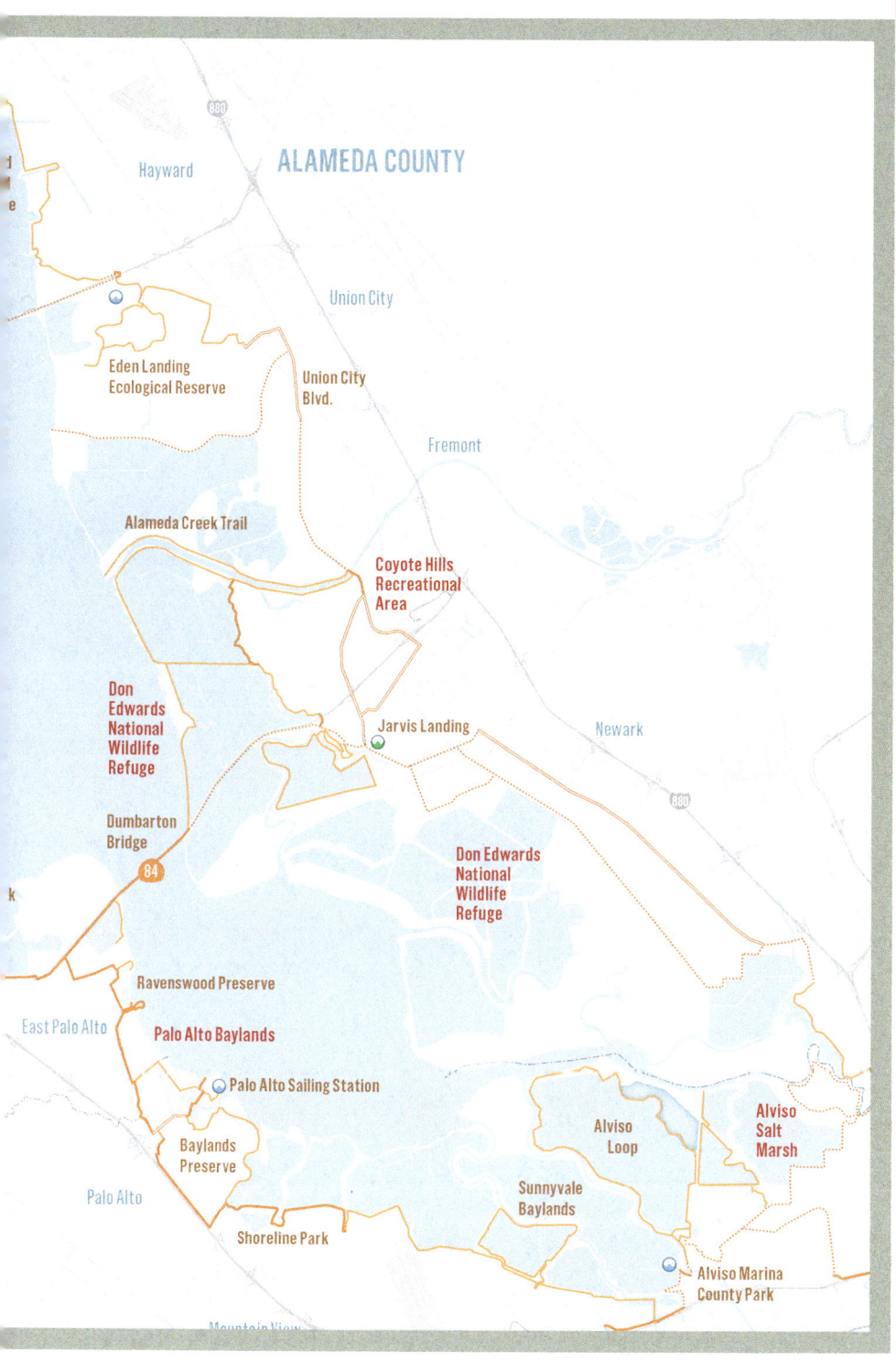

SOUTH BAY | 51

Alviso Marina County Park marsh boardwalks

Salt and Marsh Grass: Deep Breath!

- 54 // *Coyote Point Recreation Area*
- 56 // *Westpoint Harbor & Redwood City Marina*
- 60 // *Foster City: Leo Ryan Park & Baywinds Park*
- 62 // *Eden Landing*
- 64 // *Coyote Hills Regional Park*
- 66 // *Baylands to Dumbarton Bridge*
- 70 // *Alviso Marina County Park*

Did you know the South Bay Salt Pond Restoration Project will restore over 15,100 acres to a rich mosaic of tidal wetlands?"

FUN FACT

Ohlone harvested salt in the fall, scooping the fine pink crystals over the firm dry marsh to be used for preserving and medicine. Harvesting salt is still an essential bay crop, but it also preserves the salt to fresh water balance needed by our diverse sea and freshwater ecosystem. The south bay company Cargill was a leading salt producer, and once owned over 100,000 acres of Bay land.

Today, with Ohlone stewardship, we are better managing our ecosystem by reducing non native bay species.

We now face the balance of how much salt to harvest, how sea level rise contributes to warming Bay temperatures, and how marsh acreage is being replaced by new development. Salt is an essential element in the chain of bay life. Salt is necessary for brine shrimp and plankton growth. Seals eat shrimp and salty shellfish -- yet too much salt and not enough water dries up the marsh grasses. Marsh grasses serve as lungs as they filter the Bay's excess salt and oxides.

The South Bay is shallower than the rest of the Bay. Sloughs often are so sensitive to tidal flows they make it easy for seals to haul out and find restful getaways from their predators while offering abundant food such as mussels and snails. Native grass like eelgrass and cordgrass clean carbons out of the atmosphere and provide homes for mollusks and large shorebird communities. Many of the mollusks are filter feeders, eating dead fish or organic debris, algae, and bacteria.

Salt and marsh grass serve as our lungs. Scientists consider a stinky marsh the sign of a healthy Bay. Take a deep breath, marsh lungs at work!

Coyote Point Recreation Area

BAY TRAIL CARD 4

Coyote Point is an underused gem from boaters and windsurfers to beach goers and bikers. Coyote Point offers paddle rentals, an easy beach put in, and one of the most imaginative playgrounds around. The Nature Center, called the CuriOdyssey, is designed to help young children gain new scientific insights and have fun. You may want to reserve your tickets at CuriOdyssey at *https://curiodyssey.org*. The castle and dragon themed Magic Mountain for little children is not to be missed.

Magic Mountain Playground

Above: Coyote Point's bay trail. Below: Coyote Point Marina

Westpoint Harbor & Redwood City Marina

BAY TRAIL CARD 5

Westpoint Harbor is tucked behind the green glassy Google campus on Seaport Boulevard. The harbor has something for everyone: bike trails, a beautiful promenade, and centers for paddle training and sailing. It's also a prime area to view seal and wildlife. Westpoint Harbor has something for everyone: bike trails, a beautiful promenade, and centers for paddle training and sailing.

As you enter the Westpoint Harbor, you will see Westpoint Slough which feeds into Redwood Creek. Active restoration is taking place to replenish the salt marsh with Bay soil. This allows the Redwood Creek shipping channel to be used while restoration soil dredging is performed to protect marsh wetlands. Harbor seals use the shipping channel to their haul outs on Corkscrew Slough on the left and enter the Middle and Outer Bair Islands for resting, eating and pupping. Pupping season is from February through May. Salt marshes offer dense stands of reeds and salt tolerant plants trapping rich sediments for aquatic food delivery and replenishment of coastal waters. Marshes serve as a sanctuary for animals and migratory rest stops along the Pacific Flyway.

Westpoint Harbor is on the Bike Trail. Bike Trail 16 called the Bair Island Trail is a great trail to view salt marsh restoration. You can see Ridgway's rails and salt marsh harvest mice, marsh shorebirds, and the native plants that attract songbirds. Along the trail there are interesting exhibits and observation platforms.

The best observation points for seal haul outs occur in Corkscrew Slough. From the launch at West Boat Launch at Westpoint Harbor, paddle is about 1.2 miles along Redwood Creek before turning left into Corkscrew Slough. Paddle another

continued >>

Above: Dancing at the Westpoint Harbor Promenade Below: Redwood City Marina boardwalk and picnic tables

Above: California Canoe & Kayak at the Redwood City Marina which uses a private launch for skills sessions. Below: Redwood City Public Launch

1,500 feet to a PG&E pier located on Middle Bair Island. Paddle around the pier another 1,500 feet and you'll observe the seal haul outs from there to Outer Bair Island. The outer sloughs such as Steinberger Slough don't have much water in them if the lowest tide is below 4 feet, so a moderate to high tide is required for the Outer Bair Island Sloughs. This is a very tidal and muddy area so plan your trips and anticipate windy gusts in the sloughs.

Bike rentals are available in and around Westpoint Harbor. The harbor has a large parking area and offers boat storage and paddle rentals. This bustling marina is dedicated to larger boat traffic. Non motorized boats can use the beach or the low dock launch at West Boat Launch. The West Boat Launch is for designated for non-motorized boats, kayak and SUP rentals.

The **Redwood City Marina** is located just 2 miles southeast of Westpoint Harbor. New promenade, bike trail, and picnic areas are part of an expanding harbor for non-motorized boaters. California Canoe & Kayak offers kayak lessons using the shared Pioneer Fishing launch. The public launch is located 1 mile south along Seaport Boulevard in the Seaport Landing Complex. Follow

Port of Redwood City Promenade and private launch ramp.

Foster City:
Leo Ryan Park & Baywinds Park

BAY TRAIL CARD 4

There are plenty of cool activities to do in the Foster City Lagoon! When the Bay is too windy, go for a paddle inside the Foster City Lagoon.
Learn stand up paddling, kayaking, windsurfing, or rent an electric boat or a colorful paddleboat for the whole family at Leo Ryan Park in Foster City. Novice Dragon Boat Races are held here, so be on the lookout for this yearly event in June.

California Windsurfing offers beginning windsurfing lessons and rents windsurf boards, pedal boats, kayaks and standup paddle boards at the Leo Ryan Park boathouse. Edgewater Marine offers electric boat rentals. SF Bay Area Dragons offer dragon boat training.

Baywinds Park by the San Mateo Bridge is a premier windsurfing destination. The Kite School and Wind Over Water offer kiteboard lessons, windsurfing, and rentals at Baywinds Park. Bike rentals are available near both parks.

Far Left: Leo Ryan Park launch ramp next to California Windsurfing rentals. Top: SF Bay Area Dragon Boat Race from bayareadragons.org. Bottom: Baywinds Park kitesurfing

Eden Landing

BAY TRAIL CARD 8

Eden Landing is a new Bay Trail destination in the nation's first urban national wildlife refuge – The Don Edwards National Wildlife Refuge. Eden Landing is a salt marsh preserve on Mt. Eden Creek with over 1,600 acres of habitat restoration. This is a tidal area with a 1.7 mile windy paddle to the open Bay. You get a great feel of the salt marsh at these former industrial salt ponds. You can see the old salt mining structures such as housing frames, gates, and screw pumps. Laborers lived in this marsh housing and their work included using pick-axes to break up the 4-6 inch thick layer of salt from crystalizing ponds. Today, this area of Eden Landing is included within the South Bay Salt Pond Restoration Project which is returning many of the salt ponds to natural tidal marsh. This is a great place for jogging and biking with ample paths. Check the tide charts before exploring via kayak. This is a real underused natural treasure within the expanding city of Hayward. It can be pretty buggy here in the marsh, so you may want to consider using insect repellant or wear long sleeves. Bike rentals are located nearby for these gravel bike trails.

Eden Landing trail

Top: Eden Landing launches. Bottom: Avocets feed in the marshes

Coyote Hills Regional Park

BAY TRAIL CARD 8

This is a unique and significant destination point on the SF Bay Trail. Tuibun Ohlone trace their community back to this trail for over 2,000 years. The marsh ecology is a living example of salt marsh restoration, and the ADA accessibility for bikers and hikers is a great experience. Biking Bayview Trail i a flat 3.5 miles. Very accessible picnicking and camping sites through the East Bay Regional Parks District..

The reconstructed Tuibun Ohlone pit house, sweat house, and shade structure is on the Chochenyo Trail. There is an ample parking lot and many ADA and biking trails along the marshes. The main trail is ADA and side trails for biking and bird marsh observation trails parallel to the main trail along the south marsh. There are no launch areas here.
Cultural events are held June – September and include event gatherings for the local Tuibun Ohlone tribal families, tule boat building, games, and basketry. The only Tribe that has direct genealogical linkages to the intermarried Tuibun/Alson tribal group is the Muwekma. Year round park activities are usually held on weekends and include Native American history, marsh and grassland ecology.

The Bay View and Chochenyo trails offer the accessible biking and hiking connections to the Don Edwards National Urban Wildlife Refuge and the Alameda Creek Trail. At the peak of Bay View trail, you can see the white salt marshes of the south bay, the skyscrapers of San Jose, the Alameda Bike Trail, and the Coyote Hills marshes.

Top: Bay View Trail to the Nature Center. Bottom: Red Hill Trail view of the marshes

Baylands to Dumbarton Bridge

BAY TRAIL CARD 6

The greatest area of undisturbed enjoyment, whether you are biking, hiking, paddling or picnicking is found here from the Baylands to Baywinds Park. From Mountain View to East Palo Alto, the Palo Alto Baylands is one of the largest tracts of undisturbed salt and freshwater marsh in San Francisco Bay. Many consider this to be the best bird watching area for migratory birds of the Pacific Flyway in the Bay. Explore the long boardwalk that extends into the marsh, and take a few minutes to look at the interpretive displays. The Lucy Evans Nature Center offers live exhibits and docents which makes this a great shoreline adventure. The Baylands trail links to the Ravenswood Trail and the Dunbarton Bridge in Menlo Park. There are common bird sightings of egrets, plover, heron, oystercatcher, hawks, eagles and the endangered Ridgeway's Rail. Watch the blue crabs make bubbles on the marsh floor and the sandpipers catch them, or the herons wait for minutes to catch a fish. There is so much to see wherever you go here.

The salt pond floor exposes brine shrimp and clams shells. You'll see fox and rail tracks in the soft mud. You can watch the birds patiently wait for their shrimp prey in the cordgrass and pickleweed.

Look for the swallow nests under the Nature Center's roof which are filled to capacity from February to May. There are abundant walking and biking trails that begin here to connect other parts of the South and Central Bay.

While there is no paddle rental nearby, the Baylands Sailing Station is a great launch for paddle and windsurfer clubs. Paddling in the sloughs are not permitted for due to the marsh sensitivity. The Kite School and Wind Over Water offer kitesurfing lessons, windsurfing, and rentals at Baywinds Park.

Top: Byxbee Park Trails. Bottom: Baylands Park Trail

Above: Baywinds Park Windsurfing . Below: Entrance near the Palo Alto Baylands and the Lucy Evans Nature Center

Top: Palo Alto Sailing Station - great for paddlers, windsurfers, and fishing
Bottom: Bridwatching and the Boardwalk at the Lucy Evans Nature Center

Alviso Marina County Park

BAY TRAIL CARD 7

This historic town is the Bay's southernmost tip. The marina has an ample parking lot, large boat launch, and walking paths with elevated view areas. The County of Santa Clara regularly runs free salt marsh tours from May through October. The Salt Marsh Tours pontoon boat provides guided tours demonstrating the importance of salt marsh and the health of our bay. Alviso offers a flat 9 mile loop trail to view salt and freshwater ponds, and is a major rest stop for a large number of birds on the Pacific Flyway. Along the restored trail you can see some remaining buildings of Drawbridge Island in the distance. Drawbridge was originally a train conductor's overnight cabin and expanded to a town known for duck hunting. Now it is the Bay's only ghost town. Visit the Environmental Education Center for seeing wetland displays or a ride along the 4.5 mile loop trail.

Left: Alviso Salt Marsh Tours. Top: Alviso Marina County Park paddlers. Bottom: Alviso Trail along the Marshes

BUILD YOUR SKILLS

Redwood City
- California Canoe & Kayak at Redwood City Marina
- REI watersports classes at Westpoint Harbor
- Westpoint Watersports at Westpoint Harbor
- Peninsula Youth Sailing Foundation at Westpoint Harbor
- NorCal Rowing at Westpoint Harbor

Foster City (at Leo Ryan Park)
- California Windsurfing
- SF Bay Area Dragons
- Edgewater Marine
- The Kite School

Foster City (at Bay Winds Park)
- Wind over Water

Alviso
- Alviso Salt Marsh Tours

Bike Rentals available near all destinations

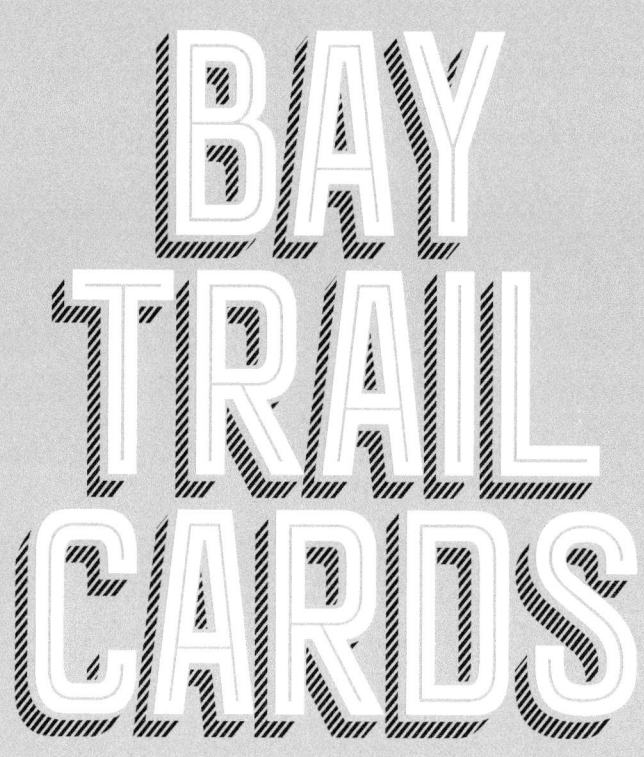

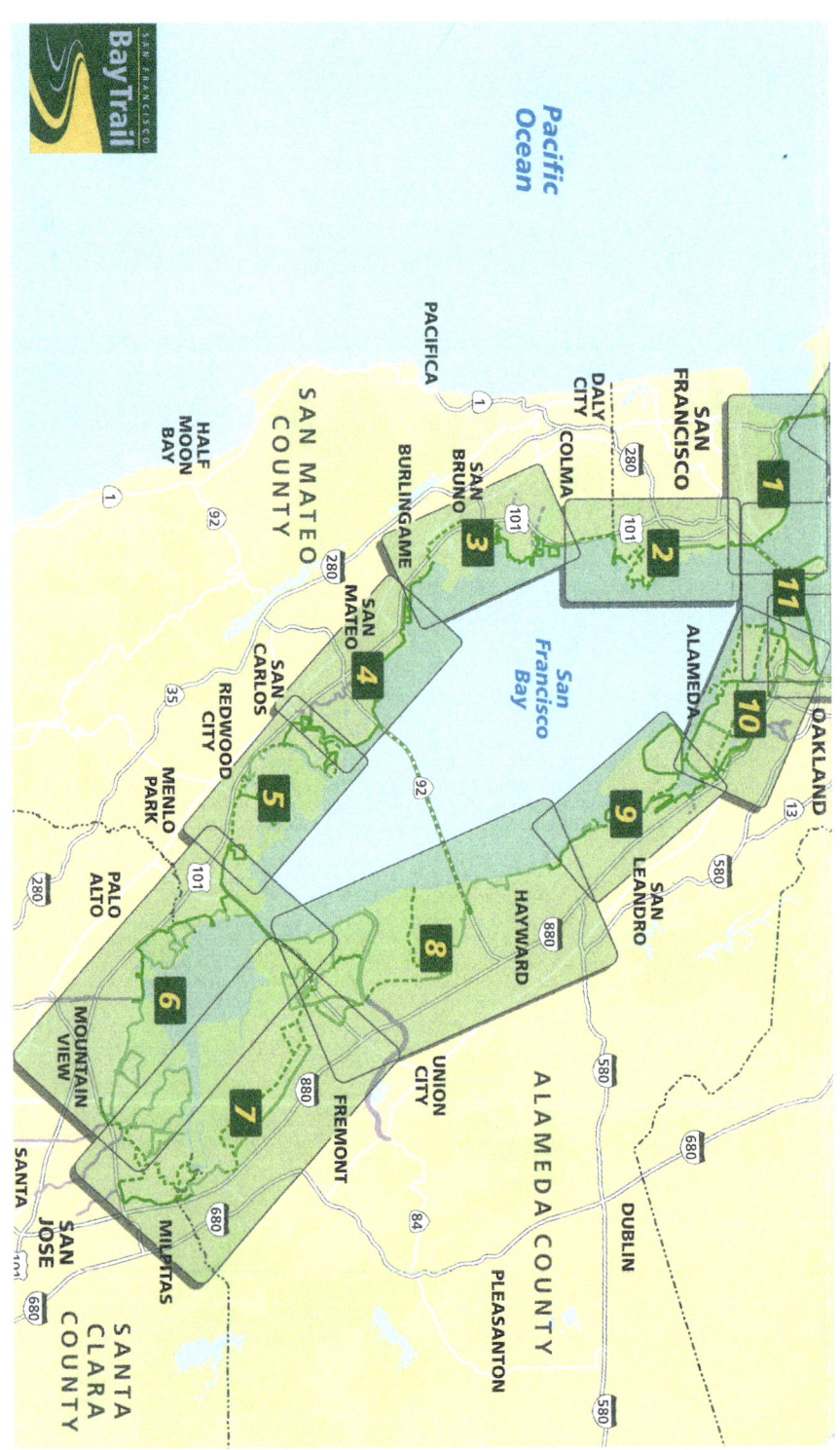

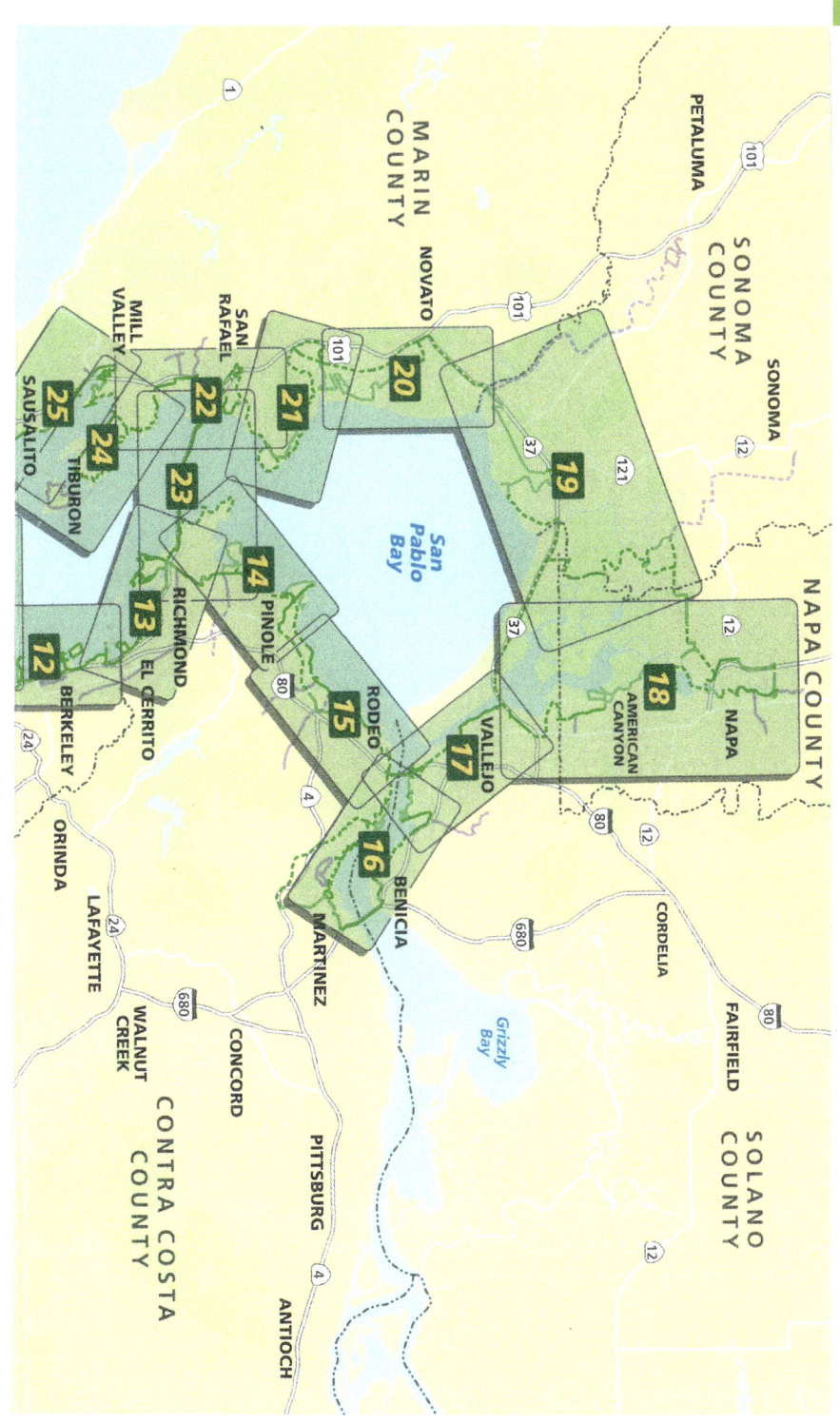

SOUTH BAY | 75

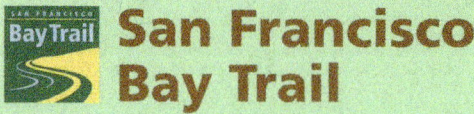
San Francisco Bay Trail

How to Use These Cards

The San Francisco Bay Trail is a bold vision for a 500-mile walking and bicycling path around the shoreline of San Francisco Bay. With these cards you can navigate over 350 miles of existing trail by bike or on foot. Whether you choose the frenetic Embarcadero in downtown San Francisco or the serene and remote San Pablo Bay National Wildlife Refuge in Sonoma, there's a card in this deck for everyone. The Bay Trail leads you to places where you can fish off piers, windsurf, swim, drop a kayak or canoe into the water, or picnic; and to shoreline towns and historic sites, museums, nature study centers, wildlife refuges, and scenic overlooks. It connects with other trails that will take you inland along creeks and streams, or into the hills and onto the Bay Area Ridge Trail, a second regional trail circum-navigating the bay along the ridgelines.

These cards begin at the Golden Gate Bridge in northern San Francisco and take you in a counter-clockwise direction around the bay through all nine counties—San Francisco, San Mateo, Santa Clara, Alameda, Contra Costa, Solano, Napa, Sonoma and Marin. The ultimate goal of the Bay Trail is a continuous path adjacent to the water. However, as the Bay Trail is a work in progress, gaps still exist in the 500-mile alignment. For example, to cross the San Mateo Bridge and to move between a few other segments, you still need to go by bus or by car. The cards show you where the trail is paved, gravel or dirt, and where the trail is on-street with bike lanes and sidewalks. The dashed lines represent incomplete, planned segments of the Bay Trail where there are no pathways, bicycle lanes or sidewalks. New segments are continuously being opened around the region, so be sure to consult www.baytrail.org for the most up-to-date information.

Where we know about dog restrictions, we have endeavored to provide that information in the text. However, we might have missed some, so please check with the city, town, county or park district that the segment runs through before inviting Fido on your sojourn. In some cases where it is possible to navigate a specific gap in the Bay Trail, our text will describe the route. However, we strongly recommend that you stay on the complete sections of Bay Trail shown on these maps. As with all segments of trail—complete or incomplete-know your limits and be courteous to fellow trail users. Never ride your bike on a sidewalk, always wear a helmet, obey posted speed limit signs, call out when passing, and always share the trail.

Key to San Francisco Bay Trail Cards

1. San Francisco Northern Waterfront
2. San Francisco Southern Waterfront
3. Brisbane Lagoon to Bayside Park
4. Anza Lagoon to Belmont Slough
5. Belmont Slough to Bedwell Bayfront Park
6. Bedwell Bayfront Park to Alviso
7. Alviso to Newark
8. Newark to San Leandro
9. San Leandro to Bay Farm Island
10. Alameda and Oakland
11. San Francisco Oakland Bay Bridge
12. Oakland to Albany
13. Albany to Richmond
14. Point San Pablo Peninsula to Point Pinole Regional Shoreline
15. Point Wilson to Carquinez Bridge
16. Carquinez Strait
17. Benicia State Recreation Area to White Slough Path
18. Northern Vallejo to Napa
19. Hudeman Slough to Black Point
20. Petaluma River to McInnis Park
21. Las Gallinas Valley Sanitary District to Point San Pedro Road
22. Point San Pedro Road to Paradise Drive
23. Richmond-San Rafael Bridge
24. Paradise Drive to Bothin Marsh
25. Strawberry Drive to Golden Gate Bridge

Disclaimer

These cards and maps reflect conditions known to their makers at the time of their creation, and reasonable steps have been taken to ensure their accuracy. Changes to the built and natural portions of the trail will occur over time. Neither ABAG nor the San Francisco Bay Trail Project makes any guarantees about trail conditions or assumes any liability for any injury or damage arising out of, or in connection with, any use of the trail or these cards and maps.

Photos
Chris Benton - card 2; Bruce Beyaert – 13; Corinne DeBra – 17;
Will Elder (NPS) – 1 & 25; Ron Horii – 7; Wilfred J. Jones – 3 & 18;
Stephen Joseph – 19; Pat Koren – 5; Tom Mikkelsen – 8, 9, 12, 14 & 15;
Karl Neilsen – 23; Palo Alto Public Art Commission – 6;
Sonoma Land Trust – box photo; Craig Solin – 24; Lewis Stewart – 16;
and Bay Trail Project – 4, 10, 11, 20, 21 & 22

1 San Francisco Northern Waterfront

Golden Gate Bridge • Crissy Field Fisherman's Wharf • The Embarcadero

Did you know that nearly the entire San Francisco bayfront is manmade? Beneath your feet lie abandoned ships, excavated hilltops, rotting piers and rubble dumped into the bay after the 1906 earthquake and fire. Above, you will find one of the world's most inviting urban waterfronts. Beginning at iconic **Fort Point** under the **Golden Gate Bridge**, follow Marine Drive southeast along the water, passing the **Warming Hut**. A natural-surface trail hugs the shoreline through **Crissy Field** along restored wetlands and sand dunes. A paved path is available inland of the marsh along Mason Street. At the yacht harbor, follow the paved trail to the east and proceed as it meanders along the shoreline through **Marina Green**, or take the spur trail to the east and see if the eclectic wave organ will play for you. Climb the hill into historic **Fort Mason**, back down to equally historic **Aquatic Park**, and continue along the shoreline to **Fisherman's Wharf**. A gap in the Bay Trail at Fisherman's Wharf means there are no bicycle lanes between Hyde and Powell streets. Head east past **Pier 39**, follow The **Embarcadero** promenade along the shoreline and stop at **Pier 7** for views of the San Francisco–Oakland Bay Bridge, Treasure Island and Yerba Buena Island. Pass the magnificent **Ferry Building**, take a trot out to the end of **Pier 14**, and continue south under the Bay Bridge. The path curves along the edge of South Beach Harbor and follows the shoreline around **Oracle Park**, home of the San Francisco Giants baseball team. Watch an inning for free from the stadium's public viewing area. The northern bayfront, as well as the city's ocean shoreline, is almost entirely within the Golden Gate National Recreation Area, the first urban national park in the U.S. See card #11 for Treasure and Yerba Buena islands.

Crissy Field & Golden Gate Bridge

Side Trip: Bike into Sausalito over the Golden Gate Bridge, see the sights, and then take the ferry back to Pier 41 in San Francisco. To access the Fort Baker Bay Trail from the east sidewalk of the bridge, use the stairs from the Vista Point parking lot and cross under the span.

2 San Francisco Southern Waterfront

Oracle Park • Heron's Head Park Candlestick Point State Recreation Area

After taking in a free inning of major league baseball at Oracle Park, take the Lefty O'Doul Bridge across the China Basin Channel onto Terry Francois Boulevard. Constant construction in this area keeps you on your toes until separated shoreline trails between the Bayview Yacht Club and **Agua Vista Park** appear, offering a look at the new Chase Center, home of the Golden State Warriors. Stop for a bite or a beverage at The Ramp restaurant, or take in the beauty of the industrial working waterfront from the adjacent pocket park. Head south on Illinois Street bike lanes or sidewalks, cross the Islais Creek Channel and turn southeast on the **Cargo Way** Bay Trail. Cargo Way ends at **Heron's Head Park**, so named for its shape when seen from the air. This odd bit of land jutting into the water was created when an additional bridge crossing the Bay was being hastily planned in the 1960's. Today it is a welcome bit of wild in the middle of the City. Before heading to the tip of the heron's beak or continuing around to **India Basin Shoreline Park**, be sure to stop at the Eco Center—San Francisco's only 100% off-the-grid building. India Basin Shoreline Park is also a potential Water Trail site, and non-motorized craft can be launched from shore. Moving south, the long-shuttered **Hunter's Point Naval Shipyard** awaits redevelopment. Once complete, the Shipyard will feature mixed-use development, new neighborhoods and open space, and over 4 miles of new shoreline Bay Trail. Currently under construction, a trail will soon encircle Yosemite Slough and connect to **Candlestick Point State Recreation Area**, California's first urban state park. Two miles of mostly paved shoreline Bay Trail meander through this oasis in the midst of the city. Until trails at Hunter's Point Shipyard are complete, use local streets to reach Yosemite Slough and Candlestick Point State Recreation Area.

Heron's Head

3  Brisbane Lagoon to Bayside Park

Brisbane • South San Francisco • San Bruno Millbrae • Burlingame

Bayfront Park in Millbrae

With **San Bruno Mountain** looming above, begin exploring northern San Mateo County at the **Brisbane Lagoon** along Sierra Point Parkway. The lagoon was a cove before Highway 101 was constructed, and it continues to support thriving bird and fish populations. Travel along bike lanes under the highway and follow the perimeter trail to **Sierra Point**, past the **Brisbane Fishing Pier** to the **Brisbane** and **Sierra Point** marinas. Continuing south along the edge of an office park, curve around **Oyster Cove Marina,** where old piers bear witness to a century of enterprise. Ships for World Wars I and II were built here, and piping was manufactured for the Hetch Hetchy, Grand Coulee, Shasta, and Folsom dams. The trail continues through **Oyster Point Park** and **Oyster Point Marina**, past **San Bruno Point Park**, the former site of one of the largest Chinese fishing camps on the bay, and across **Colma Creek**, spanned by a bicycle/pedestrian bridge. The path continues adjacent to Airport Boulevard and along North Access Road. Visit an enjoyable trail loop around a bus service facility at **Safe Harbor** and a surprising place to view wildlife. On its western side, a vibrant marsh invites shorebirds and ducks to feed. The Bay Trail is not yet complete around **San Francisco International Airport**. Aspiring pilots will enjoy the best place to view airplane landings and takeoffs at **Bayfront Park** in Millbrae. From the park, follow the paved trail south as it parallels the shoreline, edged by hotels and businesses. Continue south past the **Burlingame Bird & Plant Sanctuary**. A trail gap in this area requires bicyclists and pedestrians to use Bayshore Highway for a short stretch. When you reach **Bayside Park**, you'll see lighted fields for soccer and baseball, a playground, a dog park and lawns. Across the street on the bay is a small public fishing shore.

4 Anza Lagoon to Belmont Slough

Burlingame • San Mateo
Foster City • Redwood Shores

The section of the Bay Trail between Burlingame and Redwood Shores offers long, continuous stretches of shoreline trail. In Burlingame, begin at **Anza Lagoon**. Shortly after crossing the wooden bridge, the trail picks up again south of **Fisherman's Park** and continues into the 670-acre **Coyote Point Recreation Area**, along the edge of a golf course and through a large eucalyptus grove. Continuing south, the trail connects directly to San Mateo's **Shoreline Park**, comprised of **Ryder Park** and **Seal Point Park**. Ryder Park features an interactive tidal water system, playgrounds, a kayak and windsurf launch, picnic areas and restored wetlands. Across an elegant 105-foot bicycle/pedestrian bridge over **San Mateo Creek** is Seal Point Park, a former landfill offering expansive bay views and public art. South of the park, the Bay Marshes boardwalk extends from the trail with views of the mudflats. From here, the trail continues into Foster City, passing underneath the San Mateo Bridge, past **Sea Cloud Park** and along marshes and mudflats adjacent to **Belmont Slough**. An interior trail along **Marina Lagoon** snakes along the edge of this linear waterway. The Foster City section of the trail also connects to a bicycle/pedestrian bridge over Highway 101 that's accessed near the Belmont Sports Complex. A blue bicycle/pedestrian bridge near Oracle connects Foster City to Redwood Shores. Veer right to reach **Island Park** for a tranquil place to rest along the slough. Continue along the trail adjacent to Belmont Slough towards **Redwood Shores Ecological Reserve**.

San Mateo's Shoreline Park

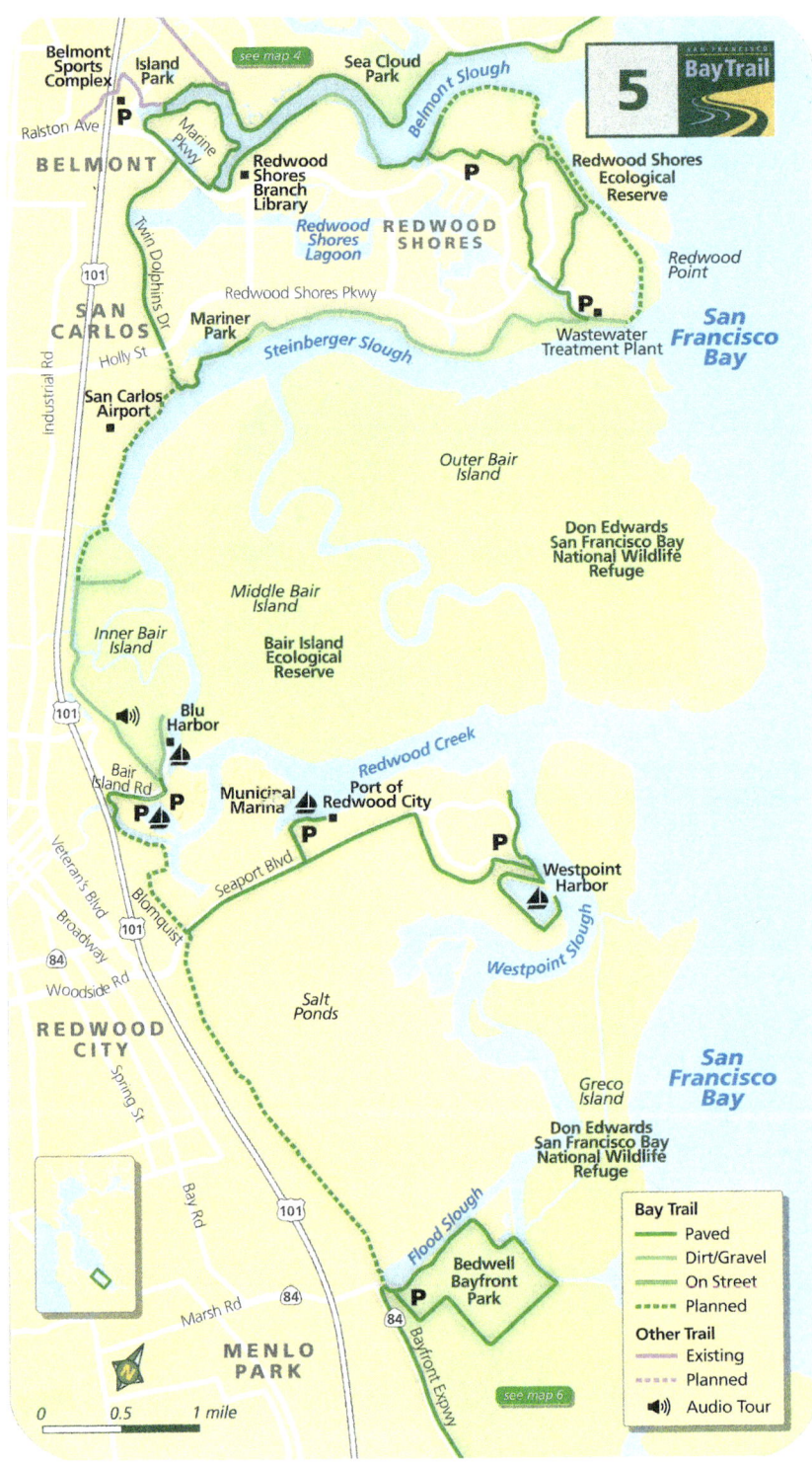

5 Bay Trail — Belmont Slough to Bedwell Bayfront Park

Redwood Shores • Menlo Park

Redwood Shores, built partly on former salt ponds, is a newer and much smaller version of neighboring Foster City. A paved trail stretches along **Belmont Slough**, passing office parks and a branch of the **Redwood Shores Branch Library**, which features interactive exhibits about the bay and shoreline habitat. At the tip of the peninsula, you'll find observation platforms for views across the wetlands of the **Redwood Shores Ecological Reserve**. Along **Steinberger Slough**, a gravel trail atop a levee stretches from a wastewater treatment plant to San Carlos Airport. At low tide, the slough transforms into a mud flat busy with feeding shorebirds. The trail terminates at the San Carlos Airport. **Bair Island Ecological Reserve** is made up of three islands: Inner, Middle and Outer. The 3,000-acre wetland complex is part of the **Don Edwards San Francisco Bay National Wildlife Refuge** and is managed by the U.S. Fish & Wildlife Service. Restoration of over 1,400 acres at Inner Bair Island to tidal wetlands is underway. A section of the Bay Trail (including a bicycle and pedestrian bridge to Inner Bair Island) has been constructed as part of the restoration. A trail along Bair Island Road leads to a bridge over **Redwood Creek**. Adjacent to Seaport Blvd, travel along the paved pathway towards the bay, past the **Port of Redwood City**, the only deep water channel in southern San Francisco Bay. At the tip of Seaport Boulevard, the trail extends around the Pacific Shores Center office complex and **Westpoint Harbor** along restored wetlands. **Bedwell Bayfront Park** in Menlo Park, a former landfill, is now a neatly contoured park with a 2-mile loop trail. From the park's top knoll, a 360-degree view awaits willing hikers. To the north and south are former salt ponds. Bayward, **Greco Island**'s marshes are part of the refuge.

Redwood Shores

6 Bay Trail — Bedwell Bayfront Park to Alviso

Menlo Park • East Palo Alto • Palo Alto Mountain View • Sunnyvale • San Jose

Beginning at **Bedwell Bayfront Park**, travel south into the **Don Edwards San Francisco Bay National Wildlife Refuge**, the first urban national wildlife refuge established in the United States. From University Avenue, the bicycle/pedestrian path on the **Dumbarton Bridge** is straight ahead. Near the bridge, a .7-mile spur trail in the **Ravenswood Open Space Preserve** hugs the edge of restored wetlands. By mid-2020, the trail will connect University Avenue to the southern section of Ravenswood Open Space Preserve and **Cooley Landing**. At the bridge over **San Francisquito Creek**, the trail splits into two different Bay Trail routes. For the shoreline route, head into the **Palo Alto Baylands** along the gravel path that leads to the **Lucy Evans Baylands Nature Interpretive Center**, Palo Alto Baylands EcoCenter and **Byxbee Park**. For the inland route, continue straight from San Francisquito Creek on the paved path and follow streets to pick up the paved path that extends along the edge of East Bayshore. Don't miss *Bliss in the Moment* a sculpture dedicated to former Bay Trail Board member and bicycle advocate Bill Bliss. In **Shoreline at Mountain View**, a paved path extends the length of the park past the historic **Rengstorff House** to the **Stevens Creek Nature Study Area**. The Stevens Creek Trail extends over 5 miles to downtown Mountain View and beyond. Follow the natural surface path behind **Moffett Field** for unique views of this former Navy facility and the wetland habitats along its edge. **Sunnyvale Baylands Park** includes acres of seasonal wetlands and grassy uplands that feature grounds for picnicking and several miles of Bay Trail. **Dogs are not allowed** in Ravenswood Open Space Preserve, Shoreline at Mountain View, behind Moffett Field and in Sunnyvale Baylands Park. **Alviso Marina County Park**, a former marina, has been restored to wetlands but you can still launch a boat here. A 9-mile dry season loop trail extends around the former marina.

Bliss in the Moment, by James Moore

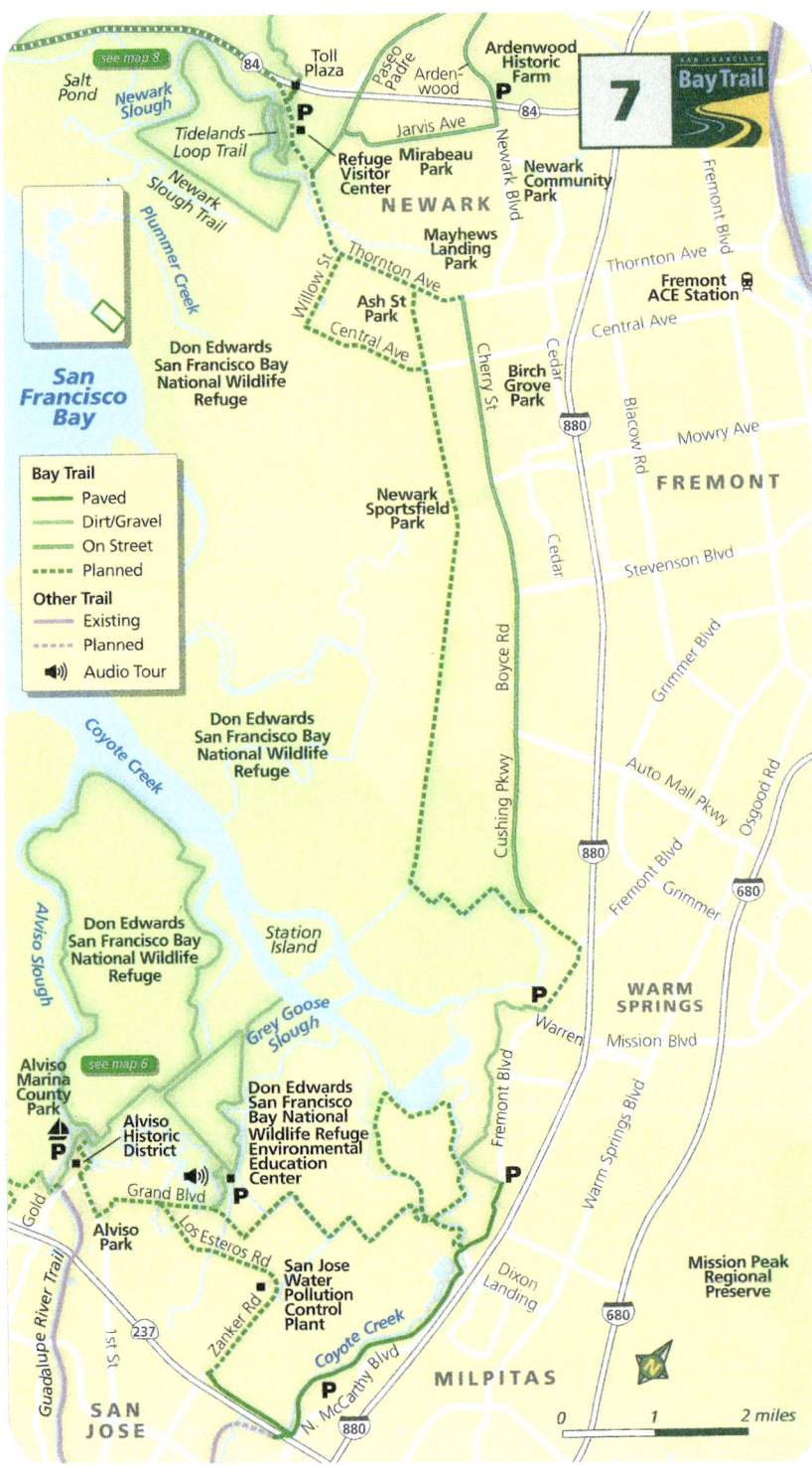

7  Alviso to Newark

San Jose • Milpitas • Fremont • Newark

A historic waterfront town at the bay's southernmost extremity, Alviso is part of the city of San Jose. The Santa Clara County Parks and Recreation Department has restored the former marina to wetlands, in addition to improving trails and constructing a boat launch at Alviso Slough. **Alviso Marina County Park** features a 9-mile dry season loop trail extending around the former marina. The trail offers views of wetlands, brackish and freshwater marshes, as well as salt ponds undergoing restoration as part of the South Bay Salt Pond Restoration Project. Visit the **Environmental Education Center** off of Grand Boulevard to view interpretive displays about the wetland wildlife and enjoy a walk or ride along a 4.5-mile loop trail encircling a restored salt pond. A path along Highway 237 provides access to the **Coyote Creek Trail** in Milpitas. This 2-mile trail follows the edge of the creek to Dixon Landing Road where the trail continues north along Fremont Boulevard, and then turns left onto a gravel levee trail that runs along the edge of the refuge wetlands. Bike lanes and sidewalks on Boyce, Cherry and Thornton streets lead through Fremont into Newark to the **Don Edwards San Francisco Bay National Wildlife Refuge Visitor Center**. **Newark Slough** curves around wetlands and meanders through the refuge's reclaimed salt ponds until it reaches the bay. The 1.3-mile **Tidelands Loop Trail** winds through uplands covered with sweet-smelling sagebrush, which offers habitat for sparrows, ground squirrels, cottontail rabbits, and gray foxes. The Newark Slough Trail branches off the **Tidelands Loop Trail** and reaches closer to the bay, circling around salt ponds for some 5 miles. Marshlands Road takes you to the Dumbarton Bridge pathway. To reach **Ardenwood Historic Farm**, follow bike lanes on Jarvis Avenue.

Alviso Marina County Park

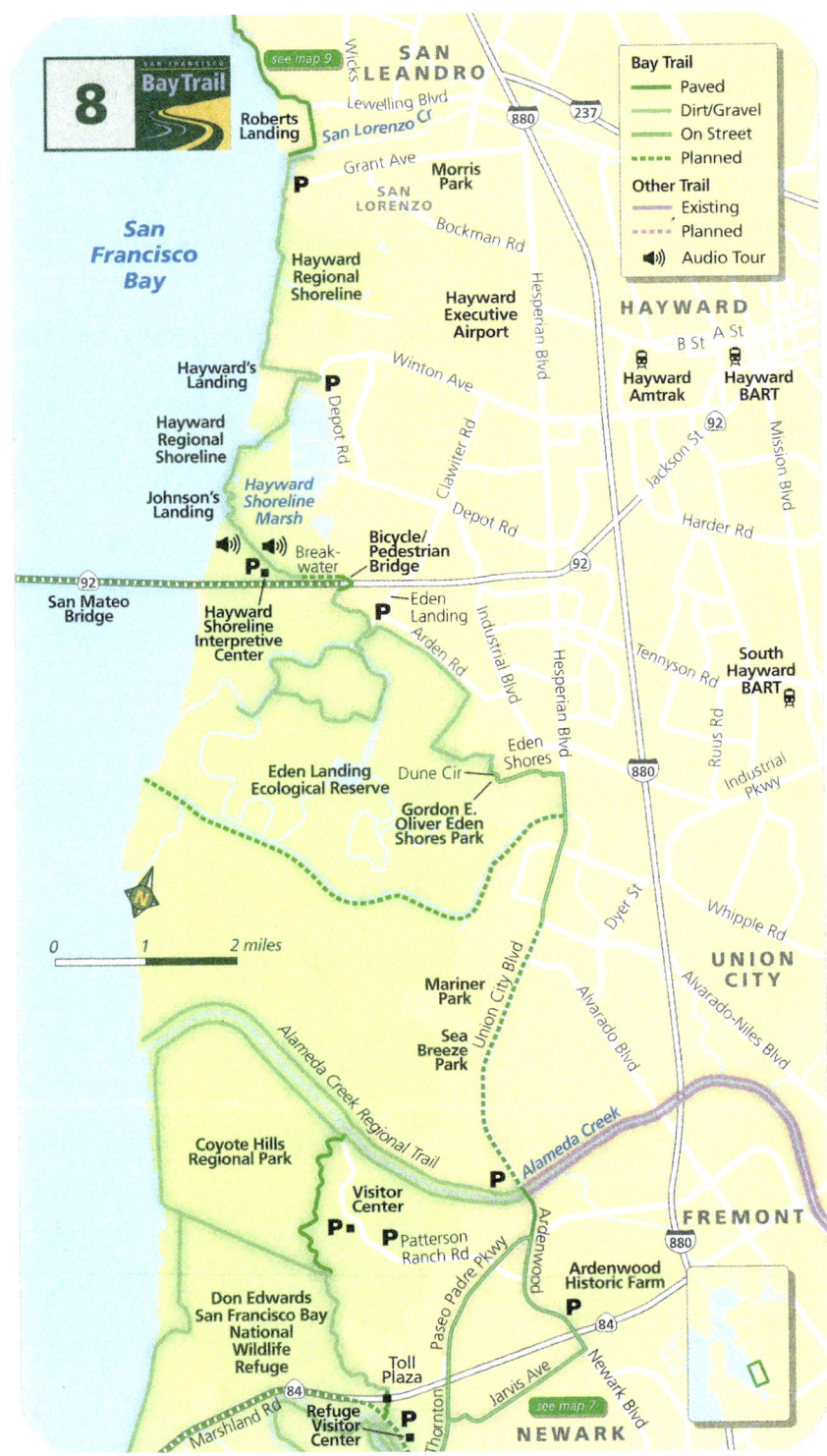

8 Newark to San Leandro

Coyote Hills • Eden Landing • Hayward Shoreline

Visit the **Don Edwards San Francisco Bay National Wildlife Refuge Headquarters** and **Visitor Center** in Newark for exhibits describing endangered species and migratory birds, and a media room with videos on the refuge and the South Bay Salt Pond Restoration Project. Cross over Highway 84 on a bicycle/pedestrian bridge above the toll plaza and head into **Coyote Hills Regional Park** to explore the maze of paved and natural-surface shoreline trails along the shallows of the bay and inland marshes. The Coyote Hills Regional Park **Visitor Center** displays exhibits on the birds, wildlife, and wetlands of the park. To reach **Ardenwood Historic Farm**, follow bike lanes along streets. Connect with the **Alameda Creek Regional Trail**, extending 12 miles from the bay to the foothills along the edge of Alameda Creek. Along the way, you'll find picnic sites and fishing ponds. To reach **Eden Landing Ecological Reserve**, turn left on Eden Shores Boulevard. The entrance is off Dune Circle near the northwest corner of **Gordon E. Oliver Eden Shores Park**. More than 600 acres of former salt ponds are being transformed

Coyote Hills Regional Park

into managed ponds and tidal wetlands in this area south of Highway 92 as part of the 15,100-acre South Bay Salt Pond Restoration Project. Cross over Highway 92 on a bicycle/pedestrian bridge and continue to the **Hayward Regional Shoreline**, stopping at the **Hayward Shoreline Interpretive Center** to view the art gallery and animal exhibits and learn about programs and activities designed to inspire a sense of appreciation, respect, and stewardship for the bay. The 1,713-acre Hayward Regional Shoreline provides habitat for hundreds of species of birds and other wildlife, including the endangered salt marsh harvest mouse. Between 1980 and 1991, 600 acres were transformed from fallow salt ponds into freshwater, brackish, and saltwater marshes. As you travel north from the Hayward Shoreline, one of the longest continuous stretches of Bay Trail guides you into San Leandro, with bay wetlands accompanying you the entire way.

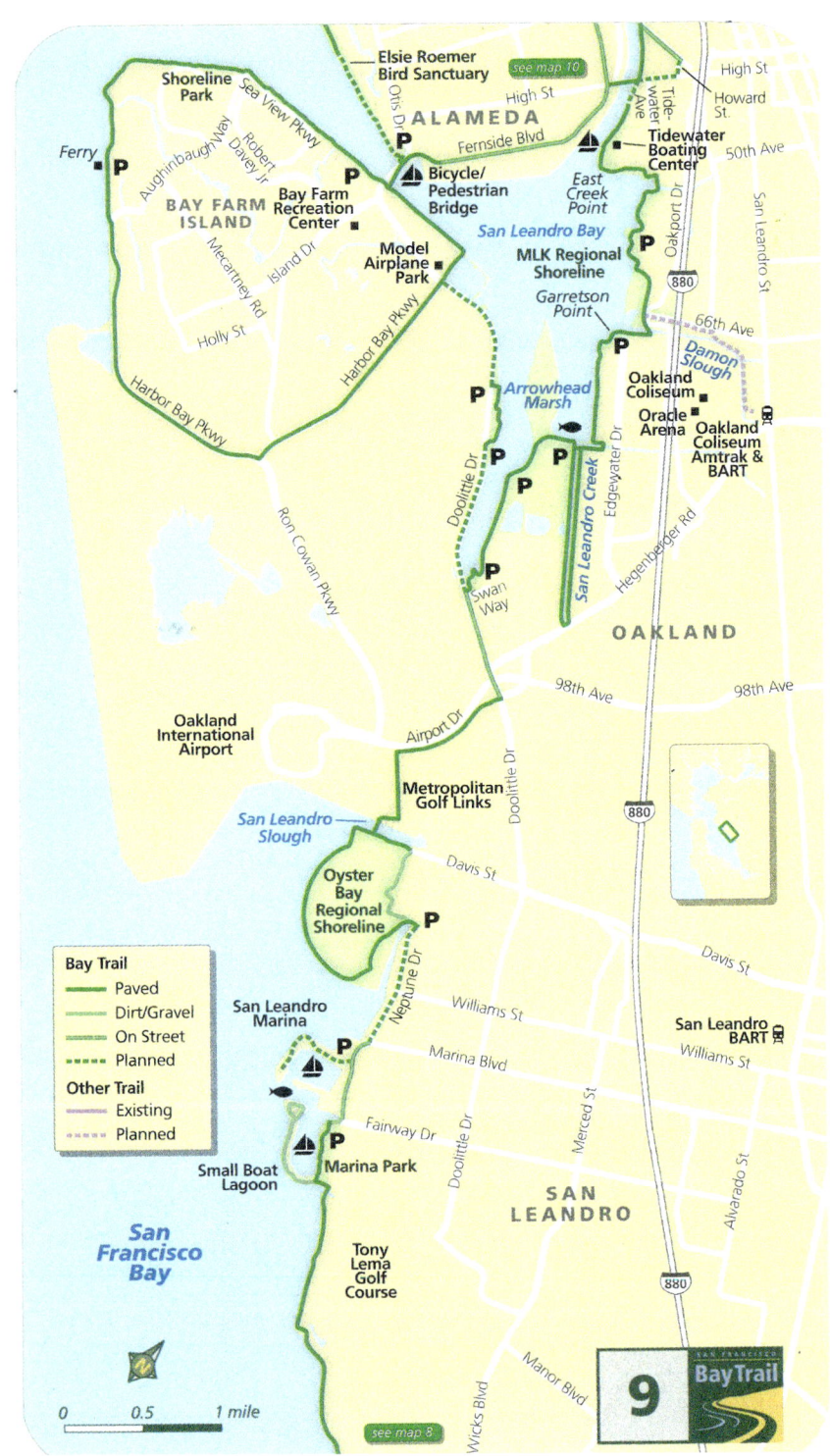

9 San Leandro to Bay Farm Island

San Leandro Marina • Arrowhead Marsh
Tidewater Boating Center

Moving north from Hayward, the shoreline becomes increasingly sinuous, urbanized, and wonderfully complex. The northern reaches of Hayward Regional Shoreline include extensive pickleweed marshes, seasonal wetlands, and acres of mudflats teeming with wading birds. The shoreline transitions to an urban environment when you enter San Leandro's **Marina Park**. Here you will find marinas, waterfront restaurants, picnic areas, a landscaped lawn, children's playgrounds and a 1-mile loop trail jutting out into the bay. Less than a mile north of Marina Park is **Oyster Bay Regional Shoreline**. Access the perimeter trail from Neptune Drive and be sure to climb the hill–there's no better spot than atop this park's summit to watch planes approaching Oakland Airport from the south. Moving north, cross the Bill Lockyer Bay Trail Bridge over **San Leandro Slough** and meander around the golf course to reach the intersection of Hegenberger and Doolittle. Using bike lanes and sidewalks, follow Doolittle to Swan Way. Veer right to enter **Martin Luther King Jr. Regional Shoreline**. This shoreline park extends along the edge of **San Leandro Bay** and forms an oasis of green surrounded by urban development. From above, the 50-acre **Arrowhead Marsh** resembles an arrowhead aimed at the heart of San Leandro Bay. Pickleweed and salt grass grow thick here, and a short boardwalk extends over the marsh. A paved shoreline trail winds along the edge of San Leandro Bay, past artwork at 66th Avenue, and continues several miles to the **Tidewater Boating Center**. Programs in competitive rowing, sea kayaking, canoeing, and boating safety are available along with boat rentals. **Bay Farm Island features** a 6-mile circular tour of this Alameda neighborhood, passing through **Shoreline Park** along the northern edge of the island. At the Harbor Bay Isle Ferry Terminal you can catch an **Alameda Bay Harbor Ferry** to San Francisco. Or, circle around Bay Farm Island and cross the Bay Farm Island Bridge, complete with a separate bicycle/pedestrian draw bridge, to Alameda. Follow cycle tracks and then bike lanes along Fernside into the heart of the city or head towards Shoreline Drive to enjoy the **Elsie Roemer Bird Sanctuary**, a shelter for ducks, egrets, gulls, and wading birds with observation from an elevated platform.

Bay Farm Island's Shoreline Park

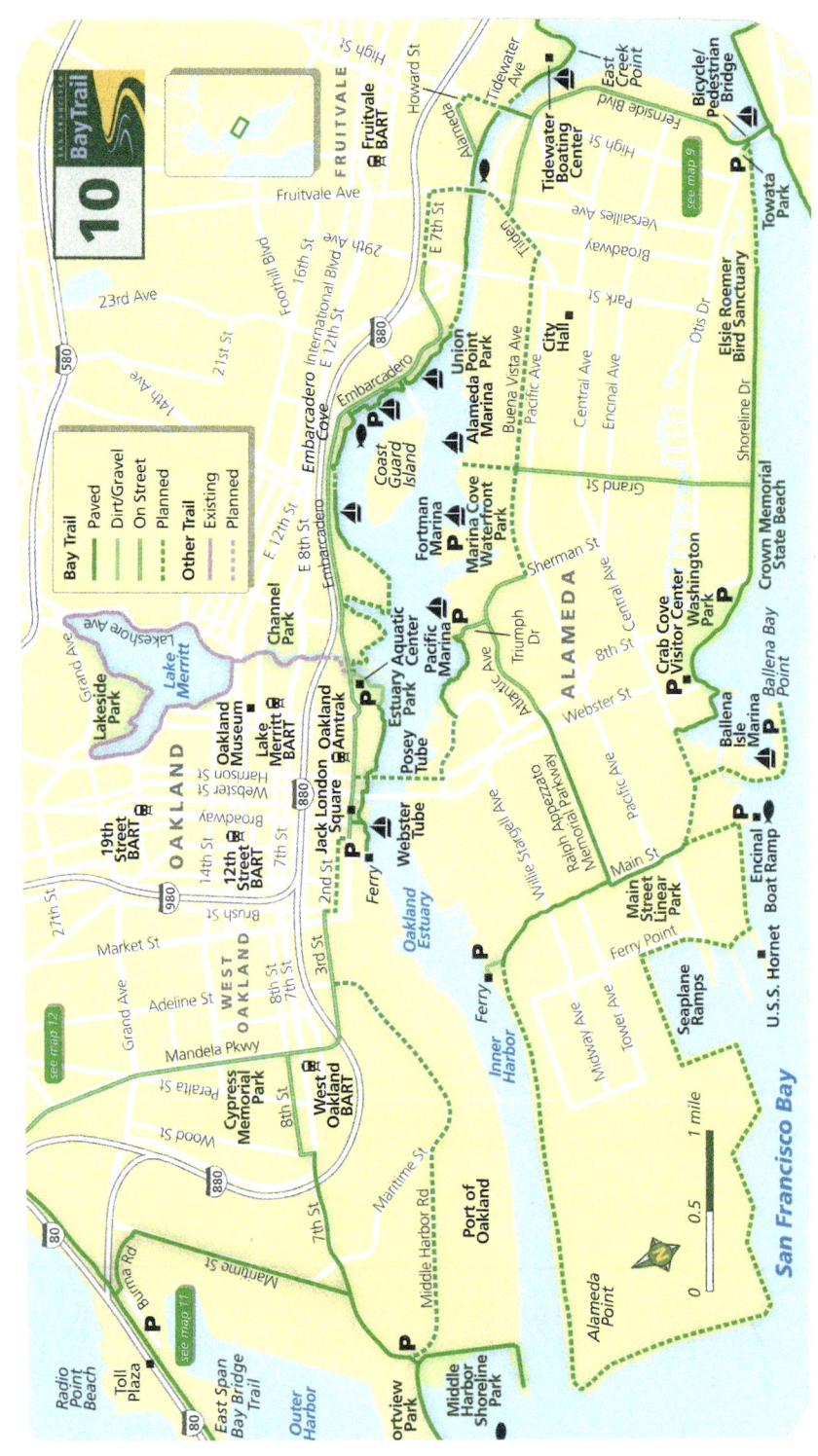

10 Alameda and Oakland

Crown Memorial State Beach • Jack London Square

There is much to discover along the Alameda and Oakland shorelines, including the bay's largest active port, beaches, historical sites and stretches of trail with delightful views. Beginning in Alameda's **Towata Park** at the base of the Bay Farm Island Bridge, enter the **Elsie Roemer Bird Sanctuary**, stopping to view shorebirds and waterfowl from observation platforms. Continue on 2.5 miles of paved trail along **Crown Memorial State Beach**, the bay's largest and warmest beach. Near McKay Avenue, you'll find the **Crab Cove Visitor Center**, a great place for kids to learn about the bay with hands-on classrooms in Crab Cove. The Bay Trail traverses **Main Street Linear Park** on the way to the **Alameda Ferry Terminal**. Although the city of Alameda has long-range plans for a shoreline trail along the Estuary, to encircle the island you will need to use city streets on the northern, eastern and parts of the western sides. Jump over to Oakland on the Fruitvale Bridge or the High Street Bridge. The **Oakland Waterfront Pathway** is a work in progress and can get complicated. The city's 19-mile waterfront is a dynamic mix of world trade and local industry, old warehouses and modern condominiums, yachts and container ships. Between High Street and Jack London Square, short segments of the Bay Trail are in place providing access to the edge of the

Oakland Estuary near Park Street Bridge

Oakland Estuary, but they are not connected. Visit the trail between Fruitvale and High streets, Fruitvale and Park Avenue, **Union Point Park**, **Embarcadero Cove**, and **Estuary Park**. Bike lanes and sidewalks along Embarcadero serve as an inland connection to some of these waterfront destinations. The trail around **Lake Merritt** is worth exploring, accessible to the Bay Trail only along city streets. There are plans to eventually connect the trails at Lake Merritt with the Bay Trail at Estuary Park. Visit **Jack London Square**, the public hub of Oakland's waterfront and learn about its rich history. Take a cruise on the **Alameda-Oakland Ferry** as it runs between Jack London Square, Alameda, and San Francisco's Ferry Building and Pier 39. To reach **Middle Harbor Shoreline Park** and **Portview Park** use bike lanes and sidewalks along city streets and be rewarded with breathtaking views. Continue north to Emeryville along city streets via Mandela Parkway or to the **Bay Bridge Trail** along the path on Maritime Street.

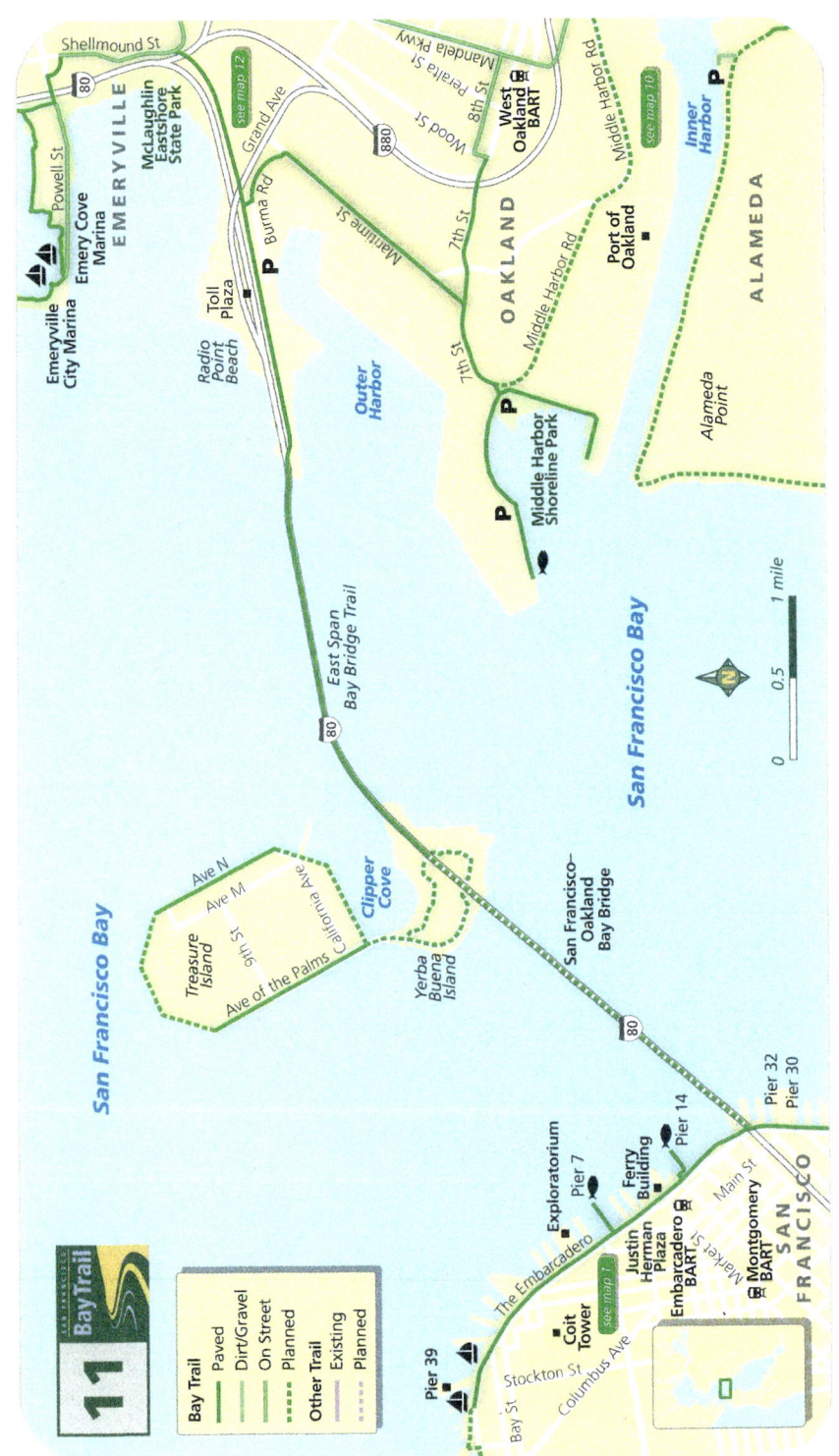

11 San Francisco Oakland Bay Bridge

Treasure Island • Yerba Buena Island

In 1955, the American Society of Civil Engineers honored the **San Francisco Oakland Bay Bridge** as one of the seven "Modern Civil Engineering Wonders" of the world. At first, the bridge carried autos on its top deck, and trucks, buses, and two tracks for the Key System rail service on the lower deck. In 1958, the rails were removed and both levels were assigned to motor vehicles.

Today, the Bay has been transformed with the new east span of the San Francisco Oakland Bay Bridge. Rising over the bay between Oakland and **Yerba Buena Island**, a self-anchored suspension span extends for 2.2 miles with a single signature tower. Following damage to the east span as a result of the Loma Prieta Earthquake in 1989, it was determined that the existing span would be completely replaced. Under construction since 2002, the new bridge opened in 2013 with a 15-foot-wide bicycle and pedestrian path on its southern edge. Take the four mile Bay Bridge Trail from the entryway off Shellmound Street in Emeryville to Yerba Buena Island and gaze up at the awe-inspiring tower of the new Bay Bridge. Work to plan, design, and complete the bicycle/pedestrian connection between Yerba Buena Island and San Francisco on the West Span of the Bay Bridge is underway. Where the bridge lands in Oakland, a future regional park, known as Judge John Sutter Regional Shoreline, is being planned to welcome travelers to the East Bay and to serve as an entry point for the bridge pathway.

East Span Bay Bridge Tower

Treasure Island was created with bay fill in the late 1930s, and was the site for the 1939–40 Golden Gate International Exposition—or World's Fair. Some 4,000 trees and 2 million flowering plants were planted for the occasion. Many of the palms and varieties of eucalyptus are still alive. Future redevelopment plans include a mix of residential, hotel, marinas, restaurants, retail and entertainment venues—plus nearly 300 acres of parks and open space. With this project, a new segment of the Bay Trail will encircle the island and connect to the Bay Bridge pathway. Two segments of Bay Trail currently exist on Treasure Island and are worth a visit.

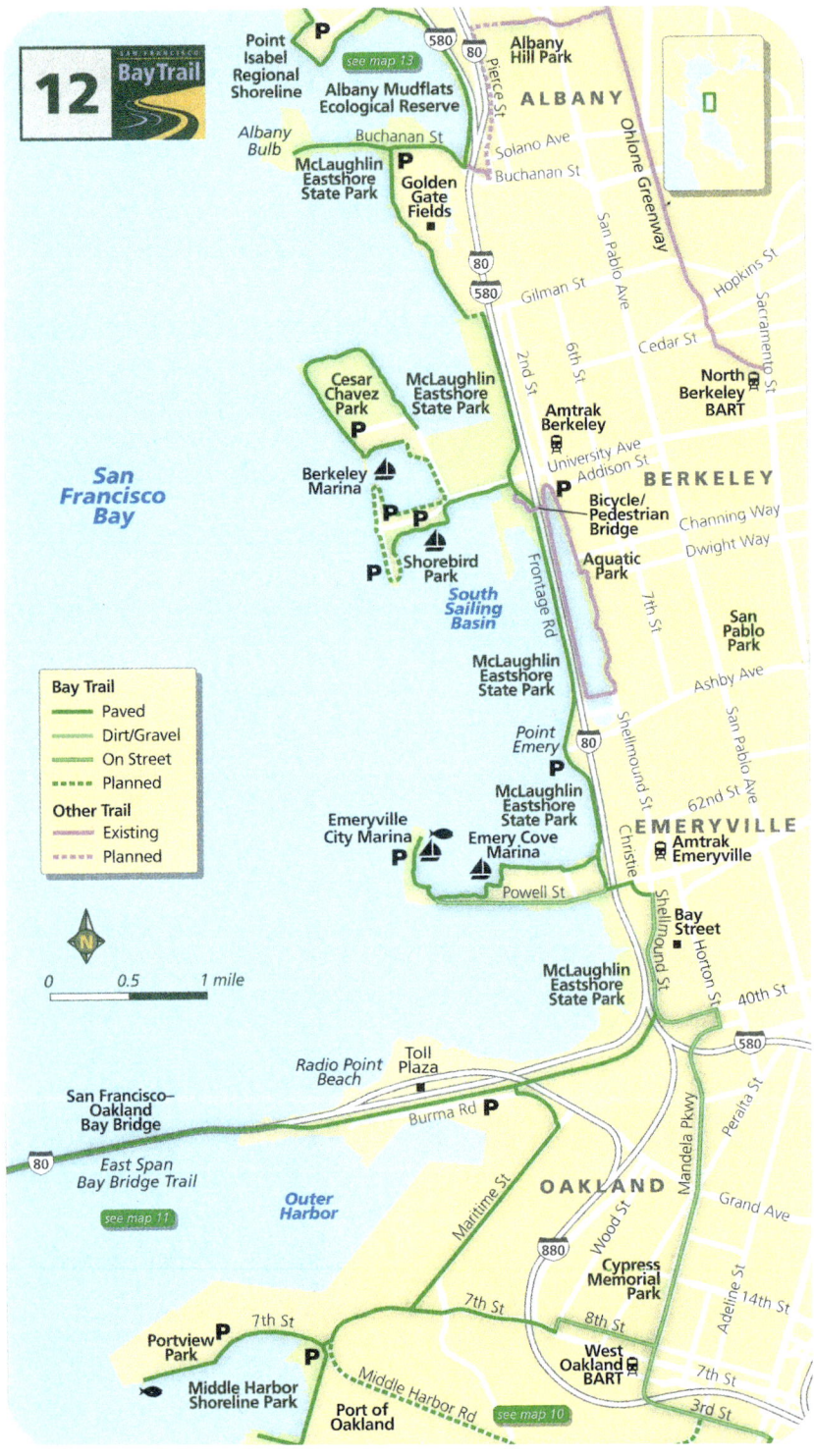

12 Oakland to Albany

Emeryville Marina
McLaughlin Eastshore State Park • Albany Bulb

In West Oakland, the Bay Trail follows streets through the busy trade and transportation zone of the **Port of Oakland**. Along 3rd Street, the bike lanes and sidewalks curve under the web of highway overpasses to Mandela Parkway. At 8th Street and Mandela, the trail splits. One leg heads towards the heart of the Port to **Middle Harbor Shoreline Park** and **Portview Park**. Breathtaking views of the Bay Bridge and the San Francisco and Oakland skylines can be seen from almost everywhere in these parks with the observation tower at Middle Harbor offering the most spectacular birds-eye views. At 7th Street, take the path along Maritime Street north through a busy port area to the **Bay Bridge Trail**. From 8th Street and Mandela, the trail route heads north along Mandela Parkway to Emeryville. Follow Mandela through the industrial zone of West Oakland, stopping to visit **Cypress Memorial Park** built in memory to those who lost their lives here in the 1989 Loma Prieta Earthquake. Mandela terminates at a shopping center; head left on Horton and left again on 40th Street to ramp over the railroad tracks. Where 40th Street turns into Shellmound Street, look for another entry to the Bay Bridge Trail to **Yerba Buena Island**. A future park, known as Judge John Sutter Regional Shoreline, will be constructed at the base of the Bay Bridge serving as an entry point to the path on the bridge. Continuing through Emeryville, use city streets to reach Christie Avenue, then take the trail along Christie Avenue and Powell Street and pass under the highway. Continue straight on Powell towards the bay to reach the **Emeryville City Marina** or turn right to follow the Bay Trail north towards Albany. This is the southern edge of **Eastshore State Park**. The trail passes **Point Emery** on its way to Berkeley, where it ducks under the **Berkeley bicycle/pedestrian bridge** over Highway 80. Take the bridge inland to visit **Aquatic Park**. Detour west along University Avenue to the **Berkeley Marina**, **Shorebird Park**, and **Cesar Chavez Park**. Rounding the edge of Golden Gate Fields, the **Albany Mudflats Ecological Reserve** is straight ahead. To your left is **Albany Bulb**, popular for its spectacular views of the bay and found art exhibits. The Bay Trail continues north squeezing between the highway and the mudflats en route to Richmond.

Middle Harbor Shoreline Park

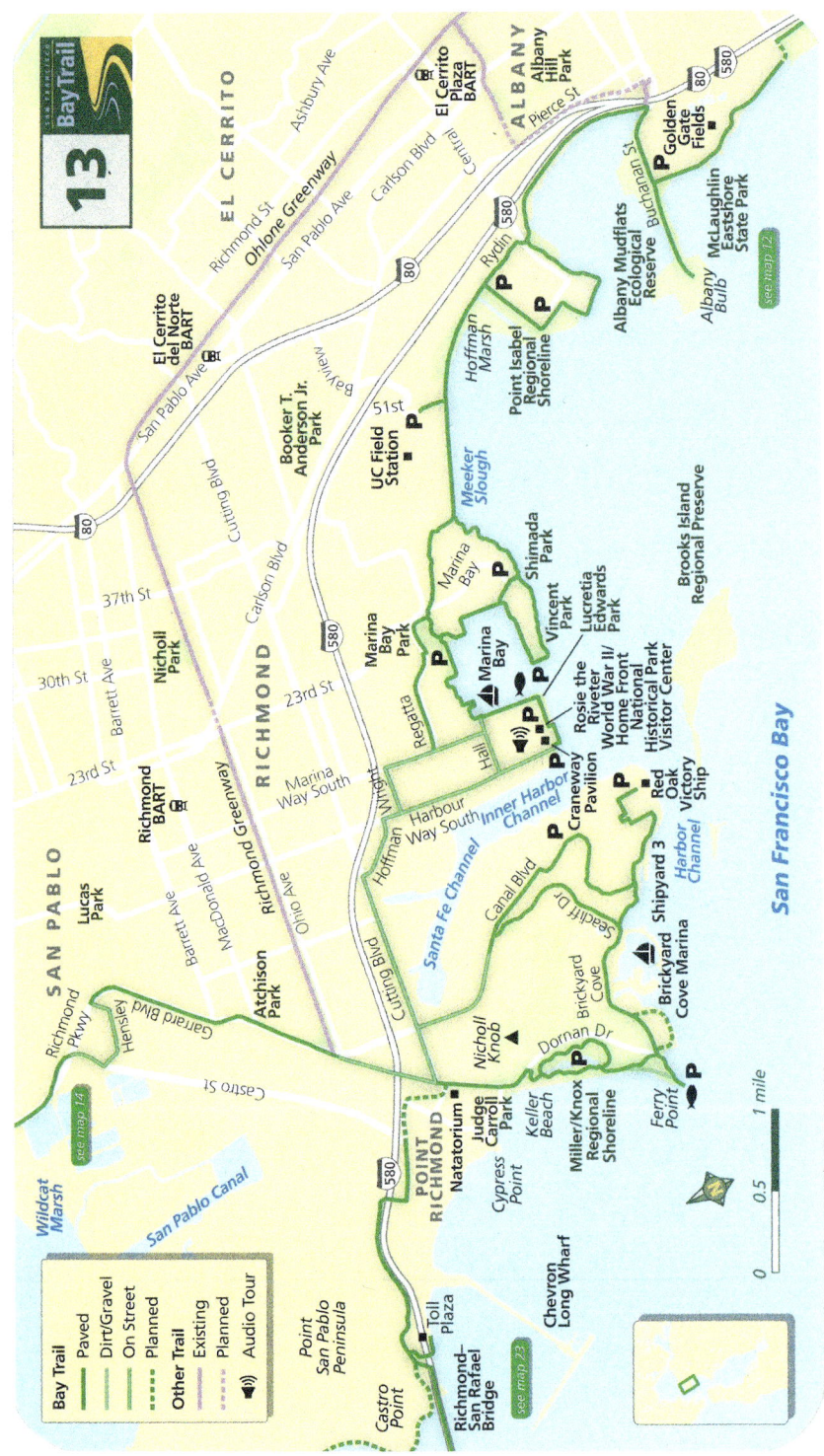

13  Albany to Richmond

Point Isabel Regional Shoreline • Marina Bay
Miller Knox Regional Shoreline

Making your way through the northern reaches of **Eastshore State Park**, round the edge of Golden Gate Fields to the **Albany Mudflats Ecological Reserve**. Visit **Albany Bulb** for its spectacular views of the bay and found art exhibits. The Bay Trail continues north squeezing between the highway and the mudflats en route to Richmond. At Central Avenue, the trail splits into two routes before reaching **Point Isabel Regional Shoreline**. Take the shoreline route for bay views and the inland route for a more direct connection. You'll have guaranteed sightings of numerous dogs running through this popular dog park. Continue along the trail between the bay and **Hoffman Marsh** to reach another trail junction at **Meeker Slough**. Take in the expansive views of the bay and wetlands rich with shorebird activity. Follow the inland route along the slough to **Marina Bay Park** and the Rosie the Riveter World War II/Home Front National Historical Park art sculpture and continue along Regatta Boulevard using city streets to reach the bike lanes on Cutting Boulevard. Take the shoreline route for expansive bay views and visits to **Shimada Park**, **Vincent Park** and **Lucretia Edwards Park** as well as Marina Bay Park and the Rosie the Riveter World War II/Home Front National Historical Park art sculpture. Visit the **Rosie the Riveter World War II/Home Front National Historical Park Visitor Center** located next to the historic **Craneway Pavillion** and follow Harbour Way South to

Trail between Meeker Slough and Shimada Park

Cutting Boulevard. The **Ferry Point Loop Trail** begins at Canal Boulevard and extends along the shoreline to Brickyard Cove Road, through **Miller Knox Regional Shoreline** and into the Ferry Point Tunnel arriving at Point Richmond. Seacliff Drive provides a shortcut to Brickyard Cove Road. Along the loop trail, visit historic **Shipyard 3** on the paved path through the Port of Richmond to the **Red Oak Victory Ship**, and stop to gaze at the San Francisco skyline. **Brooks Island Regional Preserve**, a protected nature preserve, is visible from the shoreline. Point Richmond is a great place to stop for lunch before continuing across the **Richmond-San Rafael Bridge Pathway** to Marin, or continue north along Garrard Boulevard to connect to the path along Richmond Parkway.

14  Point San Pablo Peninsula to Point Pinole Regional Shoreline

Richmond • Wildcat Marsh and Landfill Loop Trail San Pablo

Still a work in progress, the **Point San Pablo Peninsula** will someday feature a shoreline trail along the edge of this scenic peninsula to the remote **Point San Pablo Yacht Harbor**. A new trail on the **Richmond-San San Rafael Bridge** is in place for a four-year test period, so use it often to both experience a unique perspective, and to demonstrate the need for a permanent pathway! Plans are in the works for a new trail that will lead you to **Point Molate Beach Park** where you will be rewarded with views of the bridge and Mt. Tamalpais. Existing Bay Trail along the Richmond Parkway connects to the **Wildcat Creek Trail**. To get closer to the shoreline, follow the creek trail towards the bay. From the observation platform overlooking **Wildcat Marsh**, you can see a living wetland in the midst of a heavily industrialized landscape. Along Wildcat Creek east of Richmond Parkway, the first phases of the trail are in place with plans to extend from the observation platform atop the berm overlooking Wildcat Marsh all the way up to Wildcat Canyon in the East Bay hills. From the platform, you'll notice the Chevron refinery to the southwest. Continue north along the Bay Trail to the West County Wastewater District's treatment plant along the **Wildcat Marsh and Landfill Loop Trail**. This trail includes a 2.8-mile loop trail that circles a closed landfill with amazing view of Mt. Tamalpais, shorebirds and other waterfowl in **San Pablo Marsh** and Wildcat Marsh. Explore the Upper Trail for an elevated view of the marshes. Plans are in the works to connect the landfill loop trail to **Dotson Family Marsh** and **Point Pinole Regional Shoreline**, but they are not linked at this time. Access Point Pinole Regional Shoreline from staging areas off Atlas Road, Giant Highway, or at Dotson Family Marsh. The sweeping grasslands and stately eucalyptus groves of Point Pinole Regional Shoreline would be spectacular anywhere in the Bay Area, but here, along this stretch of industrial bayshore, the tranquility and recreation opportunities of this park are especially welcome. This is one of the largest waterfront parks in the entire Bay Area, with some 2,315 acres on the Point Pinole Peninsula and adjacent marshlands.

Fishing Pier at Point Pinole

15 Point Wilson to Carquinez Bridge

Pinole • Hercules • Crockett

The Bay Trail exists in isolated locations along San Pablo Bay in Contra Costa County, but you can visit several shoreline parks, large stretches of preserved marshland, and shoreline bluffs overlooking the entire bay. At the end of Pinole Shores Drive, a small parking lot marks the entrance to **Pinole Shores Regional Park**. A paved trail leaves the parking area and leads to the southwest past **Point Wilson** and also to the northeast connecting to **Pinole Bayfront Park** and **San Pablo Bay Regional Park**. A sweeping bridge provides dramatic views as it travels from the bluffs, over railroad tracks and wetlands, and lands near the shoreline at Pinole Bayfront Park where the beautiful picnic area overlooks the marshlands. Pinole Shores Regional Park will eventually be linked with **Point Pinole Regional Shoreline**. At the end of Tennent Avenue, a trail (paved, then gravel) follows the shoreline for several hundred yards and works its way around the front of the city of Pinole's wastewater treatment plant. Cross **Pinole Creek** on a footbridge and follow a paved path into San Pablo Bay Regional Park. Eventually, shoreline explorers will be able to wander unimpeded between San Pablo Bay Regional Park and Point Pinole Regional Shoreline—a stretch of some 5 miles. Across from Pinole Bayfront Park, the almost 1.5-mile **Pinole Creek Trail** stretches from the Bay Trail to Highway 80. To reach **Shoreline Park** in Hercules, continue northeast on San Pablo Avenue and take Victoria Crescent and then Victoria Park until you reach Tug Boat Lane. Some 3 miles northeast of Rodeo, on the bay side of San Pablo Avenue, is the **San Pablo Bay Regional Trail**. It consists of several miles of dirt paths winding through some 25 hilly acres, offering sweeping views of San Pablo Bay. The sole access point to this trail is difficult to find. It's off of San Pablo Avenue, at the top of a hill, across from Vista Del Rio Road. Parking here is limited; only two cars can park off-road at the access point. There is no other parking nearby. The entryway to the trail on the **Carquinez Bridge** is on the northwest corner of where San Pablo Avenue turns into Pomona Street and intersects with Merchant Street.

Pinole Shores Regional Park

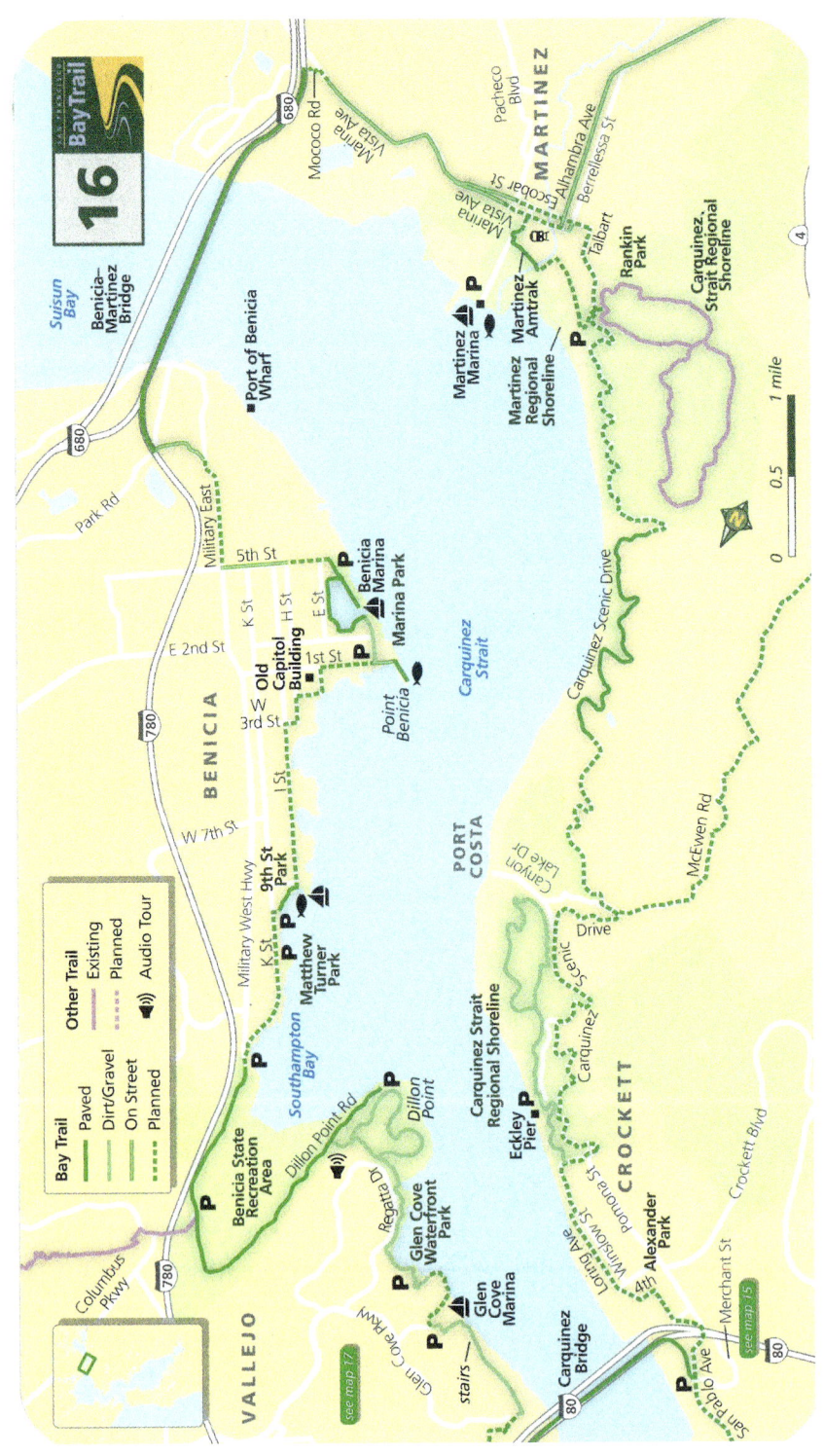

16 Carquinez Strait

Crockett • Port Costa • Martinez
Benicia • Vallejo

Where the San Francisco Bay meets the Delta, the Bay Trail will one day encircle the entire Carquinez Strait. Bookended by existing Bay Trail on the **Carquinez** and **Benicia-Martinez Bridges**, the route offers a bevy of varied sights and sounds, as well as bird's eye views of the Strait and surrounding landscape.

The pathway on the Carquinez Bridge is accessed from the intersection of San Pablo Avenue, Pomona and Merchant streets. The Bay Trail is not yet complete through Crockett and along Carquinez Scenic Drive but loop trails high above the Strait in **Carquinez Strait Regional Shoreline** offer spectacular views. Between Port Costa and Martinez, a 1.7-mile stretch of Carquinez Scenic Drive has been converted to the **George Miller Regional Trail** which provides spectacular views of the Carquinez Strait. From this trail, you can watch boats cruising through the Strait, trains running along the shore below, and hawks flying overhead. In Martinez, the Bay Trail follows city streets downtown, with a spur trail into **Martinez Regional Shoreline**. Access to the Benicia-Martinez Bridge pathway from Martinez is off Mococo Road.

Once on the Benicia side, head west on bike lanes and sidewalks along Park Road, and follow signs toward the **Benicia Marina** and downtown. Several bike lane gaps along the Bay Trail exist in Benicia, but riding on-street is not difficult for the experienced cyclist. A paved path encircles the Benicia Marina. Venture out to the tip of the **Point Benicia** (at the end of Benicia pier) before heading up 1st Street and jogging your way along residential streets until you reach the shoreline path at the end of West K. This path will take you into **Benicia State Recreation Area**, which connects on the western end to bayside trail at **Glen Cove Waterfront Park**. A lovely-if-incomplete segment of trail from the Glen Cove Marina allows hikers to scale stairs to the bluff above the bridge. To reach the Carquinez Bridge from here, use city streets.

Bay Trail on Carquinez Bridge

17 Benicia State Recreation Area to White Slough Path

Benicia • Carquinez Bridge • Vallejo

A walk through the **Benicia State Recreation Area** offers a sense of the shoreline as it was in the time of the Karkin people. Open space and natural rhythms prevail here. A paved trail leaves the eastern parking lot (off Military West) then turns into a paved trail/road at the main entrance (fee). From here you can hike, ride, or drive to the Dillon Point parking lot. To reach the point—an especially good fishing area for sturgeon, striped bass, king salmon, and flounder—walk down to the shoreline from the parking lot and follow the gravel trail for a quarter-mile. About half a mile before you arrive at the Dillon Point parking lot, the Bay Trail route veers west on a dirt trail and leads to **Glen Cove Waterfront Park**, a tranquil shoreline retreat featuring both Bay and Ridge Trail segments as well as significant Native American history. A gap in the Bay Trail between Glen Cove Waterfront Park and **Glen Cove Marina** currently requires an on-street work-around. From the Park, use Whitesides, South Regatta, Glen Cove Pkwy, and Glen Cove Marina Road to access the Marina. Amazing views of the Carquinez Straight, the **Carquinez Bridge** and the C&H Sugar facility can be had from the bluff-top Bay Trail heading west from Glen Cove Marina. This segment is a natural surface trail with stairs and is not recommended for road cyclists. To reach the Carquinez Bridge and points west via road bike, use city streets. On the west side of the bridge is the **California Maritime Academy** where officers are trained for duty on U.S. merchant ships. The academy's 7,000-ton training ship, the *Golden Bear*, is occasionally open for group tours (contact the Academy for tour info). Heading up the Mare Island Strait is where you'll find Vallejo's active waterfront, with two miles of spectacular shoreline Bay Trail and a view of the former **Mare Island Shipyard** across the channel. To reach the White Slough Path, continue on Wilson Ave (no bike lanes or sidewalks) when the pathway ends. Curve under the freeway and over to Sacramento Street where the White Slough segment begins.

California Maritime Academy

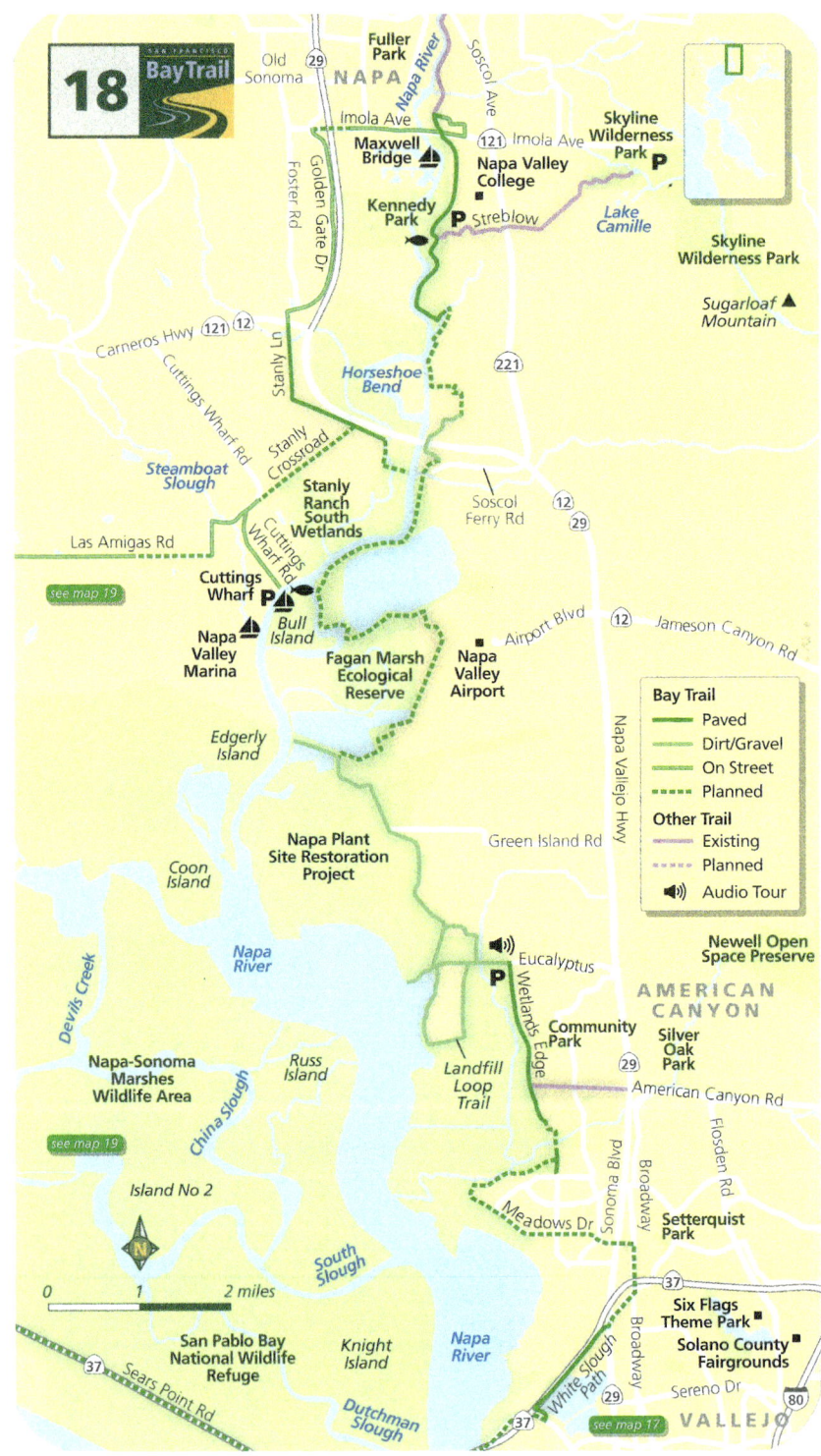

18 Northern Vallejo to Napa

Vallejo • American Canyon
Kennedy Park • Napa River

As you head north from the **White Slough Path** and into Napa County, the **Wetlands Edge Bay Trail** in American Canyon provides a bevy of birds and expansive marsh views. The **Landfill Loop Trail**, as its name suggests, skirts a closed landfill and yet allows for a beautiful and remote recreational experience. As part of ongoing efforts to restore wetland habitats around San Francisco Bay, the California Department of Fish and Wildlife completed the 1,400-acre **Napa Plant Site Restoration Project**, which included 3 miles of levee-top Bay Trail just outside the city of American Canyon. Please note that no dogs are allowed from March 2 through June 30. From **Kennedy Park**, 6.5 miles of nearly complete Bay Trail (there's a small gap on Imola at the Highway 29 entrance—use caution) exist via a combination of riverside multi-use paths and bike lanes. The Napa Valley Vine Trail—a planned 47-mile walking and cycling path from Vallejo to Calistoga—shares the Bay Trail alignment in northern Vallejo and in Kennedy Park, then continues north into downtown Napa while the Bay Trail heads west. For a trip into town or points north, continue straight under the Imola Bridge. The more rural roads of Napa County, starting at the north end of Golden Gate Drive, have intermittent bike lanes but no sidewalks for pedestrians. The **Stanly Lane** path just south of Highway 12/121, is a lovely eucalyptus-lined roadway converted to a blissfully car-free conveyance (though the pavement is a bit rough). Heading west on Stanly Crossroad through bucolic vineyards is delightful despite the lack of official bike lanes or sidewalks. Take the **Cuttings Wharf Bay Trail** down to the Napa River and launch a kayak at this designated Bay Area Water Trail site. As you head towards Sonoma County on Las Amigas Road, bike lanes end 0.75 miles after Cuttings Wharf Road. However, this remains a popular route for the more experienced cyclist.

Napa hot air balloons

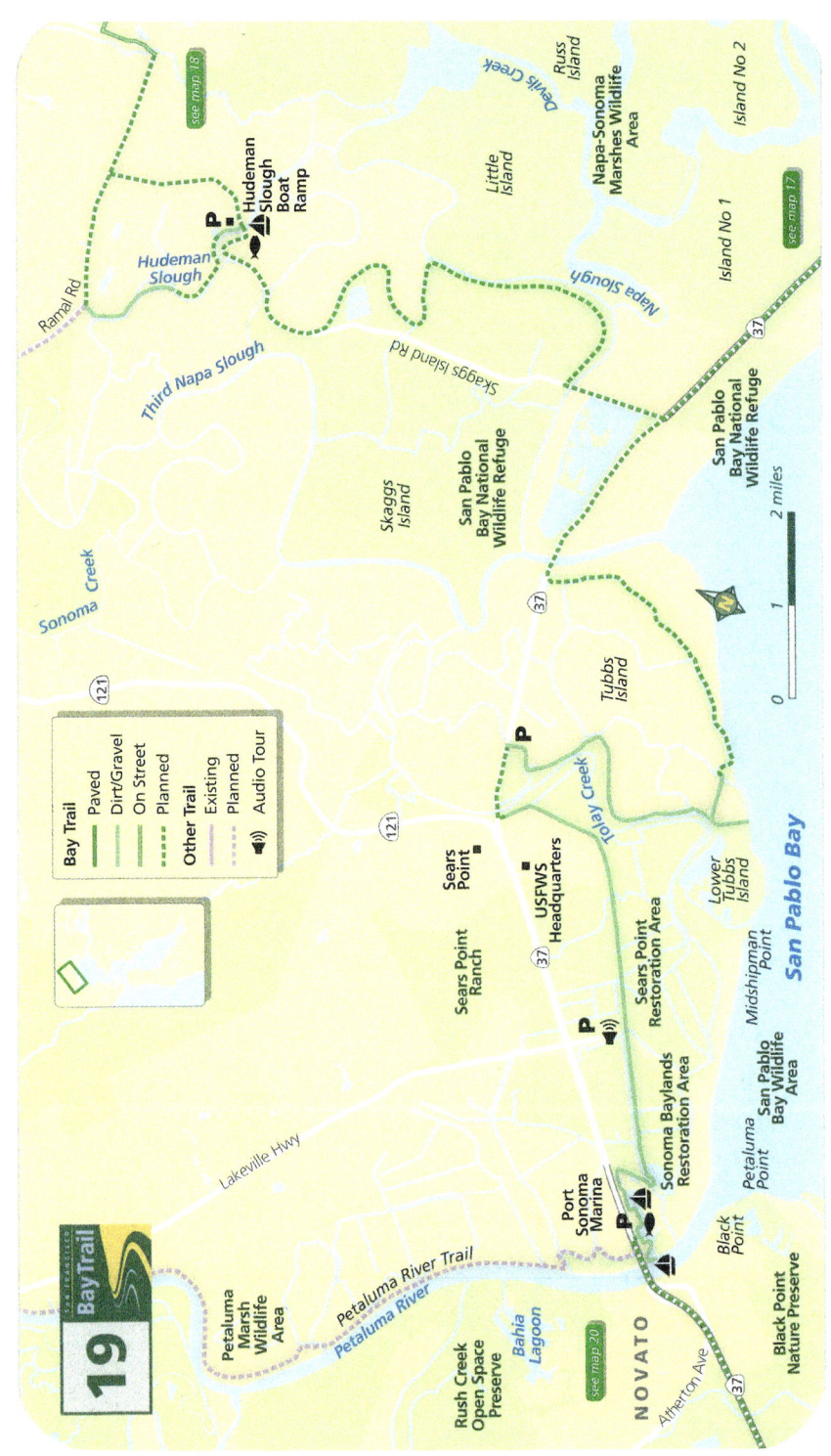

19 Hudeman Slough to Black Point

Rural Napa, Sonoma and Marin Counties

Sonoma Baylands panoramic

The northern end of San Pablo Bay is a vast expanse of marsh plain, sloughs, mudflats, egrets, herons, sandpipers avocets and more. But what about the trail? While this area represents the least complete portions of the Bay Trail system, the four segments currently open to the public—the **Tubbs Island Trail**, **Sears Point Bay Trail (Elliot Trail)**, **Sonoma Baylands Bay Trail** and the **Port Sonoma Marina Trail**—are all spectacular and should not be missed. The Tubbs Island Trail can only be accessed from Hwy 37 in the eastbound direction as a solid highway barrier prevents access to westbound travelers. From 37 East, look for the pull-out approximately ½ mile after Arnold Drive/Hwy 121 intersects Hwy 37. There is parking here for approximately 8 vehicles. This 3-mile trail once formed a loop, but several levee breaches now make this an out-and-back journey. The trail will take you to **Midshipman Point** on a levee-top, windswept, jackrabbit-laden trip to what feels like the ends of the earth. Please note that **no dogs** are allowed on the Tubbs Island trail. Driving west, turn left at the Lakeville Highway/Reclamation Road signal and look for the public parking lot a few hundred yards ahead. A dirt path parallels a paved road heading south toward the Sears Point and Sonoma Baylands levees. Once on the levee trail, head east for a 2.5 mile out-and-back (5 miles total) trek alongside a recently restored wetland-in-progress. Head west for a 1.5 mile walk or ride along the **Sonoma Baylands** marsh, created with clean dredged material from the Port of Oakland. Nearly 3 million cubic yards of clean silt were removed from the Oakland harbor to create deepwater channels for shipping. What might have gone to waste at an ocean disposal site was instead put to beneficial use in this project to restore 322 acres of diked baylands to salt marsh. Nearly twenty years on, wetland vegetation has taken hold and abundant bird life abounds. **The Petaluma River Trail** is a work in progress. While more trail currently exists at the northern end in downtown Petaluma, the trail will eventually reach the bay at Port Sonoma and connect to the Bay Trail. All of these trails are natural surface, comprised of compacted dirt or gravel.

20 Bay Trail: Petaluma River to McInnis Park

Port Sonoma Marina • Novato • San Rafael

In northern Marin County, the trail is a work in progress. The best segments of complete trail are to be found at **Hamilton**—the former Army Airfield converted to a thriving community. 650 acres of former concrete runways are now restored wetlands, with another 1,800 acres in the works on neighboring parcels. Three miles of beautiful existing levee-top trail at Hamilton can be accessed from Hamilton Parkway near Palm via the **Reservoir Hill Trail**. Access to the southernmost portion of Bay Trail at Hamilton is from Hangar Avenue near Maybeck. Park in the lot near the ballfield and walk on up to the levee trail. A formal connection south to the Bay Trail at neighboring **Las Gallinas Valley Sanitary District** will eventually be made. To access this beautiful bird-laden trail, take Smith Ranch Road to McInnis Park and follow signs to Las Gallinas. People don't normally associate sewage plants with wildlife, but Las Gallinas is a birdwatchers paradise. The trail here loops around two treatment ponds and a narrow, unpaved trail on the outer levee seems a world away though Marin's biggest city is just around the corner. A connection between Las Gallinas and **McInnis Park** is currently unavailable due to construction, but should be back by early 2021. A driving range, skateboard park, water trail launch site and country club can all be found at this county park. A parallel inland paved multi-use pathway associated with the Sonoma-Marin Area Rail Transit project—or SMART—is currently in the final design phase and will be part of the Bay Trail upon completion. When complete, the SMART pathway will run 70-miles from Cloverdale to Larkspur, over 5 miles of which will coincide with the Bay Trail.

Hamilton panoramic

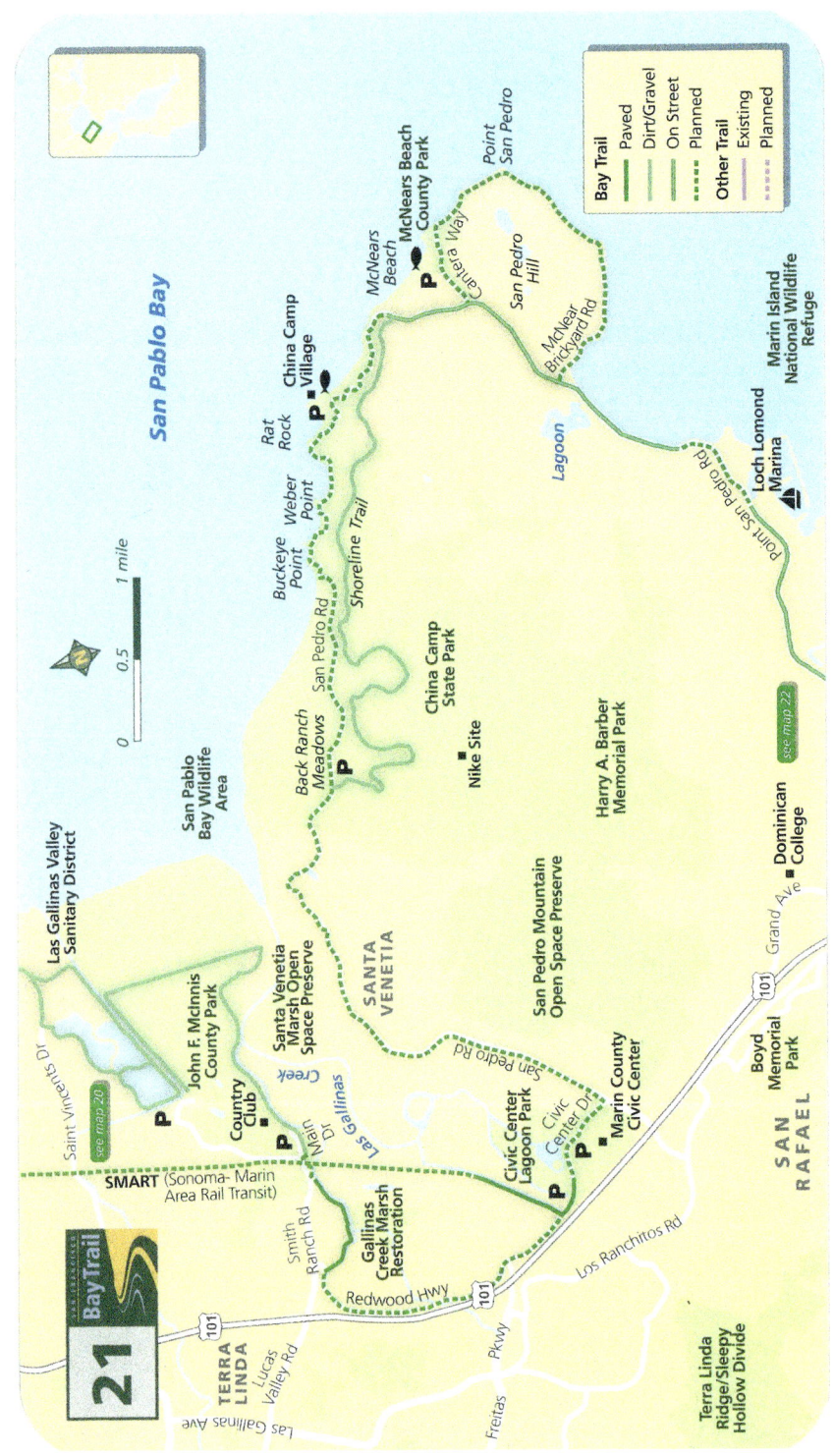

21 Las Gallinas Valley Sanitary District to Point San Pedro Road

Northern and Central San Rafael
China Camp State Park

While most people wouldn't expect to find great wildlife viewing and spectacular trails at a sewage treatment plant, that is precisely what you'll find at the **Las Gallinas Valley Sanitary District**. Located at the end of Smith Ranch Road, these 3.5 miles of trails are home to more than 185 bird species throughout the year. A direct connection to the McInnis Park Bay Trail is currently unavailable due to construction, but should be back by 2021. **McInnis Park** offers a 2.5 mile dirt loop trail and upon your return, stop in at the Country Club for a beverage.

Shoreline Trail at China Camp State Park

When entering **China Camp State Park**, the Bay Trail features two parallel routes—one on the road for experienced cyclists (no bike lanes or sidewalks here), and the spectacular wooded Shoreline Trail (3.5 miles) starting at the ranger kiosk off Point San Pedro Road. Please note that **no dogs** are allowed on Shoreline Trail, and that the park is operated by Friends of China Camp and there is a small trail-use fee. The beautiful swooping trails through China Camp's oak woodlands make it a very popular location for mountain biking. The China Camp Historic Area and museum do an excellent job of documenting the story of the Chinese shrimp camps that exported millions of pounds of dried shrimp to China annually. The historic old store is next to the beach, still open on weekends (at the time of this printing). Where this trail ends near **McNears Beach County Park**, bike lanes and/or sidewalks are intermittent leading into downtown San Rafael. McNear's is worth a visit, particularly on a hot day—a public pool, lawn, snack bar, fishing pier, and mile-long beach will entice you to relax and stay a while.

22 Point San Pedro Road to Paradise Drive

San Rafael • Larkspur • Corte Madera • Tiburon

With China Camp behind you, heading toward San Rafael on Point San Pedro Road can be a challenge as bike lanes and sidewalks are intermittent at best. While a route along the San Rafael Canal has yet to materialize, a beautiful shoreline trail begins at **Pickleweed Park** at the intersection of Kerner and Canal Boulevards. This mostly paved 2.4 mile path runs south toward the Richmond San Rafael Bridge through **Shoreline Park**. Great views of the Marin Islands National Wildlife Refuge—supporting the largest heron and egret rookery in the San Francisco Bay Area—can be had from this trail. From downtown San Rafael, the Bay Trail heads southeast from the Bettinni Transit Center. A new rail/trail associated with the SMART train will connect the transit center to the new SMART path that begins at Rice Drive, but for now, take Francisco Boulevard West to the path entrance at Rice. At Andersen, head east to stay on the Bay Trail (bike lanes, sidewalks), or continue straight to take the CalPark Hill Tunnel to Larkspur. To access the Bay Trail on the **Richmond-San Rafael Bridge** from this junction, please visit our website at www.baytrail.org as improvements are currently underway in this complex area, and conditions are changing monthly. Also see card #23—"Richmond-San Rafael Bridge." To stay in Marin, head west on Sir Francis Drake Boulevard. While there is no shoreline path around San Quentin State Prison (surprise!), a lovely bayside path begins just west of the prison at **Remillard Park** in Larkspur. Don't miss the spur that loops through the Larkspur Ferry parking lot with its unique views of the Corte Madera Creek. A new crossing of Corte Madera Creek is coming in 2021, but for now, continue west parallel to Sir Francis Drake, take the boardwalk to your left and pass under the freeway. Check out the rowing teams slicing through the waters of the Corte Madera Creek, but don't forget to turn right before the Marin Rowing Association boat house to gain access to the Bay Trail over the Creek (path adjacent to freeway). Cross back to the east side of the freeway via the bike/pedestrian overcrossing and navigate the Bay Trail gap on Redwood Highway until you reach the shoreline path at Redwood and Nellen. Sit a spell at Muzzi Marsh, a part of the **Corte Madera Marsh Ecological Reserve**—it's a veritable bird-palooza! Continuing south on Paradise Drive is not recommended for pedestrians as there are no sidewalks and a minimal shoulder. This segment is also not recommended for inexperienced cyclists. It is, however, highly recommended for cyclists who are comfortable with rural winding roads, oak forests and stunning bay views.

Sir Francis Drake statue at Remillard Park in Larkspur

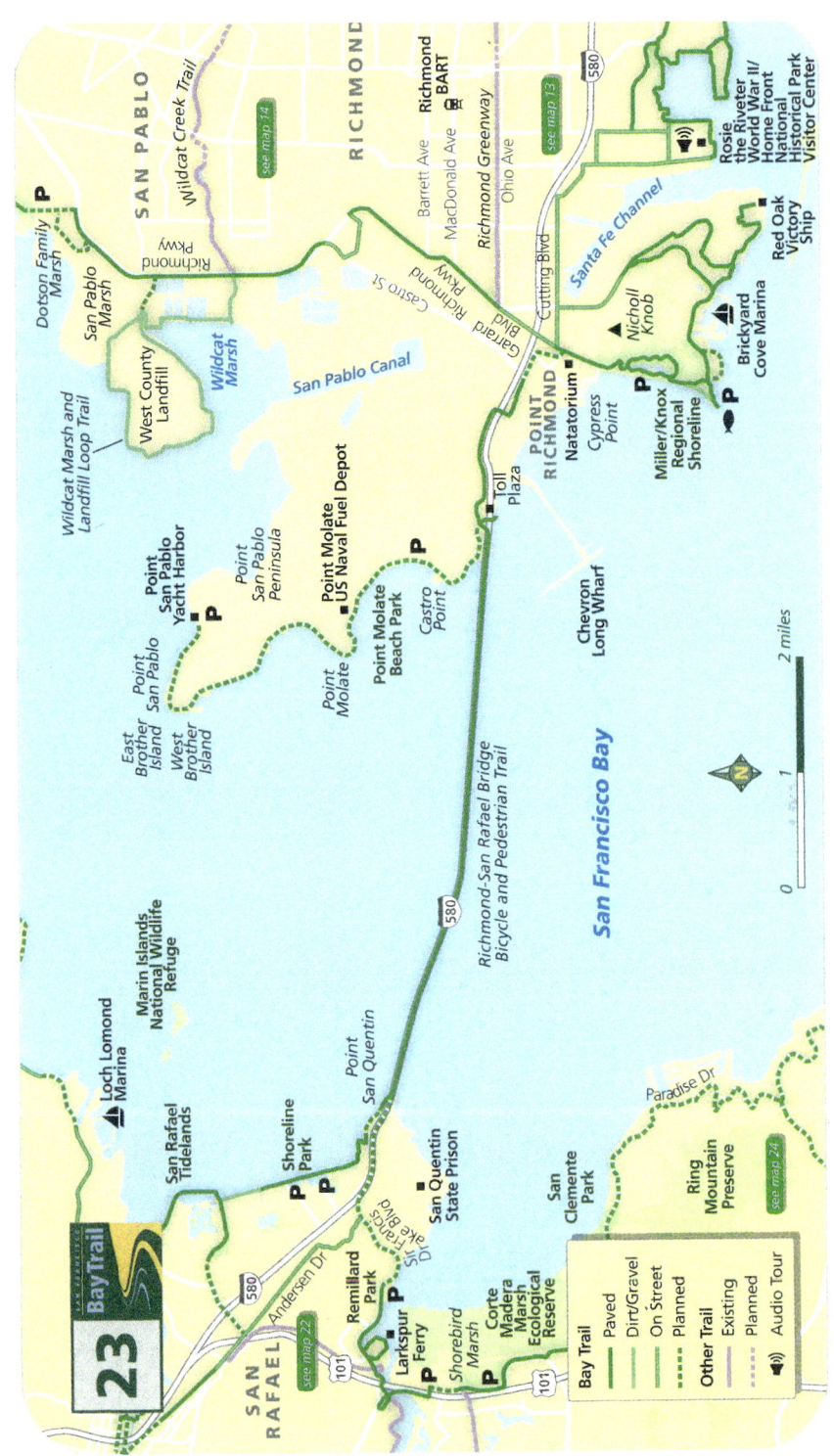

23 Richmond–San Rafael Bridge

Bicycle and Pedestrian Trail

In the fall of 2019, the San Francisco Bay Trail was thrilled to add a 4.5-mile separated pathway for cyclists and pedestrians on the upper deck of the Richmond-San Rafael Bridge, connecting trail users in the counties of Marin and Contra Costa for the first time in the span's 64-year history. Advocates first began requesting a path for cyclists and walkers several decades ago. After much work on the part of groups like the Marin County Bicycle Coalition, East Bay Bicycle Coalition (now named Bike East Bay), TRAC (Trails for Richmond Action Committee), San Francisco Bay Trail Project and countless others working with elected officials and agencies on both sides of the bridge, a four-year pilot project began with much fanfare on November 16th, 2019. Automated bicycle and pedestrian counters have been installed on both sides of the bridge. The number of bicyclists and walkers that use the trail will help to determine if this pathway becomes permanent, is removed, or is only available to trail users during limited hours or days of the week. For this reason, it is important to show your love for the new pathway by riding or walking it early and often! Scenery from the span is spectacular, providing views of East Brother Island, Point Molate, Point San Pablo, Red Rock Island and Mt. Tamalpais. New pathways with wayfinding signage leading up to the bridge on the Richmond side make access simple and straightforward. From the intersection of Garrard Boulevard and Richmond Avenue follow the signs and travel through the streets of Point Richmond to the Richmond-San Rafael Bridge trailhead at Castro Street and Tewksbury Avenue. Improvements from the Marin side are underway. From the Larkspur Ferry, take the Bay Trail adjacent to Sir Francis Drake Boulevard heading east. The pathway ends before the San Quentin Prison gate and bikes and pedestrians must share the road shoulder (no bike lanes or sidewalks exist here) for 1.5 miles then exit at San Quentin, hang a quick left on Main Street under the freeway, then the path will be on the east side of the bridge at the Main Street/Francisco Boulevard East/I-580 intersection.

Improvements on Francisco Boulevard East and on the Sir Francis Drake/I-580 flyover are underway at the time of this printing. For the most up-to-date info, look for this card (Richmond-San Rafael Bridge card #23) on the Bay Trail website, www.baytrail.org.

Richmond-San Rafael Bridge

24 Paradise Drive to Bothin Marsh

Corte Madera • Tiburon
Angel Island • Mill Valley

Heading south down the Tiburon Peninsula on **Paradise Drive** is a beautiful section of road with great views and low traffic volumes. Be aware, however, that no path, bike lanes or sidewalks exist on Paradise Drive. While the Paradise Loop is a spectacular local favorite among cyclists, it is not recommended for pedestrians or families cycling with young children. **Paradise Beach Park** (fee) is an ideal location for picnicking, fishing off the pier or just plain relaxing. Paradise Drive culminates in downtown Tiburon. The **Angel Island and San Francisco ferries*** dock off Main Street, at separate piers. Head north on bike lanes or sidewalks until you reach Mar West Street near Town Hall, and look for the entrance to the multi-use path on the left. Situated on an old railroad alignment, this is some of the most spectacular Bay Trail in the nine-county Bay Area system. From Mar West, the multi-use path extends approximately 3 miles, ending at **Blackie's Pasture**. Be sure to visit the statue of Blackie the horse–Tiburon's most famous resident. Where the trail ends in Blackie's Pasture, experienced cyclists and adventurous pedestrians should look for the bicycle/pedestrian cut-through on the northwest side of the parking lot. Take Greenwood Beach and Greenwood Cove roads parallel to Tiburon Boulevard. Just before Greenwood Cove Road intersects Tiburon Boulevard, across from the gas station, there is an older, narrow walking path that winds pleasantly along the shoreline. Cross a small bridge and head up Harbor Cove Road to Strawberry Drive. Note that from the end of the path at Blackie's Pasture to Strawberry Point there are no formal bike paths or lanes, and sometimes no sidewalks. To find a hidden gem of shoreline spur trail at **Strawberry Point**, take Harbor Point Drive off of Strawberry Drive through an apartment complex. The adventurous will be richly rewarded.

Picnic on Tiburon Ridge

*****Side Trip:** Grab your bike or your boots, a picnic lunch and board the ferry to Angel Island. Circumnavigate the island on a combination of paved and hard-pack dirt roads and trails. You can also take the ferry to San Francisco and ride the Bay Trail from Pier 41 or the Ferry Building, across the Golden Gate Bridge and back into Tiburon.

25 Strawberry Drive to Golden Gate Bridge

Mill Valley • Tamalpais Junction • Sausalito

To find a hidden gem of shoreline spur trail at Strawberry Point, take Harbor Point Drive off of Strawberry Drive through an apartment complex. Strawberry Drive turns into Seminary Drive where bike lanes and a dirt sidepath await. Seminary Drive ends at Redwood Highway and yet another gap in the Bay Trail for bikes. For pedestrians, a natural surface path parallels Seminary and Redwood—bikes should remain on the (busy) street. Once on the west side of the freeway, an older narrow asphalt path can be found along the shoreline. Continue towards **Bayfront Park** on Hamilton Drive. Pedestrians can make a shoreline loop detour by taking Shelter Bay Avenue. Access to Bayfront Park and the **Mill Valley Sausalito Path**—another fine example of a rail-to-trail conversion—begins across from the police station. This trail along **Bothin Marsh** offers a great bird-and-people watching experience. The lycra-clad road-riding set whizzes by while parents teach kids to balance on their bikes, and herons, sandpipers and egrets troll the mudflats for tasty treats. The **Tennessee Valley Path** is an important connector trail heading west to the Pacific Ocean, Golden Gate National Recreation Area and the Bay Area Ridge Trail. The Mill Valley Sausalito Path ends as you enter Sausalito, but bike lanes and sidewalks bring you into a thriving downtown*. Heading up toward the **Golden Gate Bridge** on Alexander Avenue, the bike lanes disappear for a stretch before you turn right on East Road (bike route #5) toward Fort Baker. An active military post from the 1850's to the 1990's, **Fort Baker** glistens with history. To reach the bridge, follow Conzelman Road under, around, and up to the west parking lot. Depending on the time of day and day of the week, bikes may need to be walked down the stairs and across to the east sidewalk.

Fort Baker, Golden Gate Bridge

*Side Trip: Take the ferry to San Francisco and ride the Bay Trail from Pier 41 up the San Francisco waterfront, across the Golden Gate Bridge and back into Sausalito. To access Fort Baker from the east sidewalk, use the stairs from the Vista Point parking lot and cross under the span.

SF BAY AND WATER TRAIL RESOURCES

SAN FRANCISCO BAY TRAIL INFORMATION

San Francisco Bay Trail Project www.baytrail.org
Metropolitan Transit Commission www.mtc.ca.gov
State Coastal Conservancy www.scc.ca.gov
San Francisco Bay Water Trail www.sfbaywatertrail.org
Association of Bay Area Governments www.abag.ca.gov

PUBLIC TRANSIT

511 www.511.org
Up to date transit, rideshare, and biking
Transit&Trails www.transitandtrails.org
A website to assist your hike, bike, and trail planning using public transit
Buses & Trains www.clippercard.com
Use Clipper Cards for all of the following
Alameda County Transit Authority www.actransit.org
Bay Area Rapid Transit (BART) www.bart.gov
Caltrain www.caltrain.com
Napa Valley Transit www.nctpa.net
San Francisco Municipal Transit Agency (MUNI) www.sfmta.org
San Mateo County Transit District www.smctd.com
Santa Clara Valley Transportation Authority www.vta.org.ca.us/transit
Benecia Transit www.ci.benicia.ca.us/transit
Vallejo Transit www.vallejotransit.com
Sonoma County Transit www.sctransit.com
Union City Transit www.union-city.ca.us
West Contra Costa County Transit www.westcat.org
California Bay bridge bicycle shuttle service www.dot.ca.gov/dist4/shuttle

Credits: Ben Botkin, Daniel Garepis-Holland, Kel O'Donnell Ginther, Janai Southworth, East Bay Regional Parks District, San Mateo County Parks

ACKNOWLEDGMENTS

We gratefully acknowledge the media images and guidance of:

Ben Botkin
Water Trail Planner
San Francisco Bay Water Trail
San Francisco Bay and Water Trail photographer
Metropolitan Transportation Commission
https://mtc.ca.gov

Corrine DeBra
San Francisco Bay Trail Tour Guide
www.walking-the-bay.com

East Bay Regional Parks District
https://www.ebparks.org

Daniel Garepis-Holland
SF Bay Transit and Aerial Photographer

Greater Farallones National Marine Sanctuary Visitor Center
https://farallones.noaa.gov/education/visitorcenter.html

Sally Holland
SF Bay Photographer and Editor

Kel O'Donnell Ginther
SF Bay Nature Photographer

Valentin Lopez
Tribal Chairman, Amah Mutsun Tribe
http://amahmutsun.org

Charlene Nijmeh
Tribal Chairwoman, Muwekma Ohlone Tribe
http://www.muwekma.org

San Mateo County Parks Department
https://parks.smcgov.org

Janai Southworth
SF Bay Plankton Research Scientist
Discord: *Pacific Plankton*
Instagram: *pacificplankton*

Laura Thompson
San Francisco Bay Trail Project Manager emeritus
Metropolitan Transportation Commission

INDEX

10 *Angel Island*
12 *Bay Model*
66-69 *Baylands Park*
60-61 *Baywinds Park*
66-67 *Byxbee Park*
40-41 *Brooklyn Bain*
40, 58-59 *California Canoe & Kayak*
60 *California Windsurfing*
38-39 *Candlestick Point*
12 *Cass Gidley Marina*
14-15 *China Camp*
64-65 *Coyote Hills Regional Park*
54-55 *Coyote Point Marina*
34-35 *Crissy Field*
44-45 *Crowne Beach*
12 *Dunphy Park*
44-46 *East Bay Regional Parks*
62-63 *Eden Landing*
36-37 *Embarcadero*
44-45 *Encinal Beach*
60-61 *Foster City*
36-37 *India Basin*
40-41 *Jack London Square*
60-61 *Leo Ryan Park*
66-69 *Lucy Evans Nature Center*
14-17 *McNears Beach*
11 *Mount Livermore (Angel Island)*
20-21 *Napa*
20-21 *Napa River*
32-33 *National Marine Sanctuary*
66-69 *Palo Alto Baylands*

18-19 *Petaluma*
18-19 *Petaluma River*
34-35 *Pier 52 (San Francisco)*
22-23 *Point Pinole Regional Shoreline*
56-59 *Redwood City Marina*
56-59 *Redwood City Public Launch*
24-25 *Richmond Ferry*
42-43 *San Leandro Marina*
18-19 *San Pablo Bay*
12-13 *Sausalito*
12-13 *Schoonmaker Point*
12-13 *Sea Trek*
60-61 *SF Bay Area Dragons*
60-61 *The Kite School*
10-11 *Tiburon Ferry*
42-43 *Tidewater Center*
12 *Turney Street Boat Ramp*
56-57 *Westpoint Harbor*
60-61 *Wind Over Water*

31901067464455